BURNS MONUMENT, CALTON HILL, EDINBURGH

Rome Wasn't Built In A Day

THOUGH you should "Strike while the
   iron is hot"
And "A stitch in time saves nine,"
"Rome," so they say, "wasn't built in a day" —
   A great immortal line.
I'm not saying that in this rat-race tedium
   Time is there to waste,
But you'll never strike a happy medium
   If your life is lived in haste.
So, though "the early bird catches the worm"
   And others you could quote,
In the hectic rush hour,
   They often miss the boat.
For sometimes the slow ones win the race,
   As I'm sure you are aware,
Remember the lovely story of how
   The tortoise beat the hare?
So though "make hay while the sun shines"
   May be your steadfast motto,
There'll always be a next time
   Along life's pleasant grotto.
Let life not be a humdrum race
With troubles overfilled,
It's time you realised that Rome
   Took more than a day to build.

Linda French.

People's Friend Annual

●

CONTENTS

SCENIC VIEWS   J. Campbell Kerr   BACK COVER   Tarr Steps, Exmoor.

Hang The
Expense

F RANK LATHEM pulled his fiancée to a halt outside the travel
agent's window. "Doesn't it look great? All that blue water with
the sun shining on it . . . and the parasols . . . Don't you just
wish you were sunning yourself right now?"

Bernice Rothwell tucked her scarf more cosily round her neck and
shivered.

"Brrr! At this moment a bit of sunshine would be heavenly. But don't
you try to get round me. There are lots of lovely beaches around
Britain. We don't have to spend all that money just for a beach."

"There's the sun, lovely and hot, shining all day long," Frank
tempted. "Wouldn't you love to go somewhere like that? It's not as if
we hadn't got enough money saved."

Bernice stopped him there. "Saved, Frank. Saved for *after* our
honeymoon."

She turned to face him. Standing very close, the top of her head was
about level with his chin and she had to tilt her face to look up at him.

"We'll have a lovely honeymoon wherever we go, I'm sure. But
honcymoons are only the beginning; our marriage is to last for ever."

"Darling." Frank's arms came round her, holding her close as he
kissed her parted lips. "I want that, too. Of course I do. And I realise
you're right to plan for the future, but you've never had a holiday
abroad.

"I know camping was fun for you all, when you were young, but that's
probably the sort of holiday we'll have to have, once we start a family. I
would like to have spoiled you a bit, just this once."

"There'll be time for such things before we have any babies. Right
now, with the house and furniture and everything, we need every
penny."

She kissed him quickly to soften the blow. "Anyway, what you've
never had you never miss — isn't that what they say?"

But it's not true, Bernice thought, her eyes sliding to the numerous
posters in the travel agent's window.

Frank was right. The Rothwell family holidays had been fun, but they
hadn't been luxurious. Most of her school friends had flown to Spain
and Greece, some even further afield, and she had often listened to
them talking with a slight twinge of envy.

I suppose I was lucky coming last in the family, she thought, recalling
some of the tales she'd heard about the deprivations of those earlier
years.

by
MARGARET
JOHNSTON

Carol and Alan had been born soon after their parents were married and there'd been little money to spare for anything while Mr Rothwell was just beginning his sales career. Bernice had arrived when Alan was nearing 12 and, though he and Carol were already needing school uniforms, their father was well up the career ladder and earning quite well.

Now, Dad is sales manager, and Mum doesn't have to worry about every penny she spends, Bernice thought. She talks of those days as if they were fun, but I know they couldn't have been. No-one likes being short of money and Mum is so happy now that she's got nice things about her. And Dad's loving the thought of giving me a grand wedding without having to worry about how much it's costing.

At the thought of her coming wedding Bernice squeezed Frank's hand where it lay round hers in the pocket of his sheepskin jacket. He looked down at her lovingly.

"Only three more months, darling."

"Three months and four days," Frank told her. "Three months, three days and eighteen hours, to be exact."

"Are you sure?" Bernice calculated rapidly. "Yes, you're absolutely right.

"Oh, I do love you, Frank. You're not like a lot of men, staid and stuffy and unromantic. June's boyfriend only makes jokes about their wedding. I'm sure he wouldn't know to the minute when they are to be married."

"Ah! If I'd known you wanted it to the minute —" Frank brought her to a halt again as he raised his wrist, pretending to check his watch.

"Idiot!" Bernice laughed fondly. "I didn't mean you to reckon it up. I was just saying how lovely it is that you care about such things."

"I care about mortgages and fuel bills, as well," Frank said, a little indignantly, as if he fancied she was accusing him of being frivolous.

"Of course you do. But just now and then you forget them and would go absolutely crackers if I didn't stop you."

"Would you call it being crackers if I suggested a nice hot cup of coffee?" Frank asked.

Bernice pretended to consider the matter seriously. "I think the exchequer might even stretch to a hamburger," she said, straight faced.

But when they got inside the warm café with its smell of fried onions and wet clothes, Bernice suddenly discovered she didn't want to eat. She was glad of the coffee and cupped her hands round the cup, letting its warmth soak into her.

"Roll on summer," she said feelingly.

FRANK watched her closely as she lifted the cup to her lips. Her face looked pale and it wasn't like her to refuse food. When she shivered and he heard the cup rattle against her teeth, he drank his own coffee quickly.

"Come on," he said masterfully, getting to his feet. "I'm taking you right home. You look frozen. How do you feel?"

"Frozen," Bernice answered, a slight smile on her lips. It didn't reach her eyes, however, and she leaned against Frank as they walked out into the street.

Casting one look towards the bus queue, Frank walked across to the taxi rank. It was a measure of how ill Bernice was feeling that she didn't protest.

"I'll get her right to bed," Mrs Rothwell told him quarter of an hour later. "I thought she looked under the weather this morning, but she would insist she was all right."

"I'll ring tomorrow, love," Frank whispered as he leaned over the bed, but Bernice was almost asleep.

MRS ROTHWELL answered Frank's call next day but she advised him not to come round. "Bernice isn't too bad, but there's no sense in you catching the flu — if you haven't already. The doctor says she'll be fine in a couple of days. She sends you her love."

"Give her mine," Frank said disconsolately.

He would have liked to go to see Bernice but he supposed Mrs Rothwell was talking sense. He certainly didn't want to take time off work with all the expense of their new home ahead.

That day seemed longer than most and, when at last it was time to leave for home, his thoughts turned to Bernice. Or rather, to the lack of Bernice, and how empty the evening would seem without her.

DEAR COMPANION

FRAIL old lady handling a sturdy stick. Too heavy for her? A climber's staff, companion of her late husband's over many a mountain track. Bruised on many a traverse over scree.

Now he is gone. Home is the stick, home from the hill. Silent in the hall, it guards the memory of one whose strength so fortified his wife.

But now it's on the road again, in the fragile hand of his widow learning slowly to use her hip re-replacement.

"Try this lighter stick," they all advise. "It will be easier to handle, and still give you support."

"I'll use my husband's stick," the old lady replied. "It will give me also moral support!"

Rev. T. R. S. Campbell.

As he was going towards the bus stop he caught sight of a large display of flowers in a shop window.

Someone, somewhere would love some flowers from you, one notice said, while another assured him that: *Flowers tell her you love her.*

Frank paused. Ever since he and Bernice became engaged, they'd been sensible about money. Their budget was carefully calculated to let them save as much as possible.

Just this once, he told himself, he wasn't going to be sensible. He made up his mind to take the plunge.

He walked into the shop a little diffidently. The smiling assistant soon put him at his ease.

"I don't know what she'd like best," he explained, nodding to the notices. "We're getting married soon and, and — well — perhaps you'd advise me."

"Red roses," the girl said without hesitation. "They mean I love you. Flowers have meanings," she explained when Frank looked puzzled. "The language of flowers."

"Then red roses it must be." He grinned. "A lot."

He felt his cheeks grow hot, but the girl seemed to find nothing silly in his request. She wrapped the bunch carefully and handed it over.

Frank was a little dismayed when she told him how much they cost. Not because he begrudged Bernice anything, but because he knew what she'd say about such extravagance.

When he got to Bernice's house he gave the flowers to Mrs Rothwell, who exclaimed with delight.

"She's asleep now, but I'll put them in water, near her bed, so that they'll be the first thing she sees when she wakes up.

"She's had such a long sleep, I'm sure she'll be feeling better. And when she sees these . . . ! They're beautiful!"

A S her mother had planned, Frank's flowers were the first thing Bernice saw when she woke from a refreshing sleep. The rest, the numerous hot drinks and the doctor's medicine, seemed to have done the trick and already she was feeling much better.

She saw the roses and thought she recognised her mother's artistic fingers in their arrangement.

"Bless you, Mum." She smiled, when her mother came into the room a little later. "I'm fine now, there's no need to keep running up and downstairs."

"Keeps me slim." Mrs Rothwell laughed, handing her yet another mug of steaming liquid.

"Remember when we were little? You used to give us Grandad's old walking stick so we could knock on the floor when we wanted you because you didn't always hear us if we shouted."

"Remember! I should say I do! Thank goodness you weren't sickly children, or you'd have had me worn to a shadow. 'M . . u . . . m! What can I do?' 'Mum, I want a drink.' 'Mum, I've read all my comics.' 'Mum . . .' "

"Can I come downstairs?" Bernice finished for her. "Can I?"

"Oh, I don't know. Later, then. Just give me time to tidy up and then I won't need to keep going in and out making draughts. Now drink up," she urged.

"Bossy!" Bernice told her, but she smiled and Mrs Rothwell smiled back. They both knew there was no further need for words.

Listening to the sounds of her mother tidying up downstairs, Bernice lay back against the pillows, her eyes straying to the vase of flowers. They really were quite beautiful. They must have cost a fortune, she thought.

How like her mother. She'd always liked to give them treats, even when they were quite small. Just little things, but it must have been a struggle to find even those extra coppers for a comic to cheer up a convalescent.

If there'd been flowers then, they had been picked from the garden. Or even just a few twigs of evergreen if there was nothing else, but still showing their mother's concern for them.

It made the gifts no less thoughtful because they had cost so little. Even now, the value of the flowers didn't matter, though the fact they had cost her mother a lot of money brought a warm feeling to Bernice's heart. Mum loved having money to spare, and she couldn't resist spreading this happiness around her family.

When Mrs Rothwell finally allowed Bernice downstairs, she took the vase with her.

Her mother smiled, hurrying to take them from her and put them on the table beside the couch.

"Sit there, love." She tucked a rug over Bernice's legs before turning to smile at the flowers. "Red roses for a blue lady," she hummed.

"It's a song," she explained, seeing her daughter's enquiring look. "Or it was, when I was a girl. 'I want some red roses for a blue lady. Send them to . . . di-da-di-da-di-da.' "

"Oh, Mother! You never can remember words, can you?"

"Well, it was a few years ago. More than a few," she added ruefully. "Anyway, it fits. I was feeling blue. Thanks, Mum."

"What?" Mrs Rothwell looked puzzled. "I didn't get them. They were from Frank.

"Red roses mean I love you. Surely you know that? That was what the song was all about. Something about sending them to the one I love."

"You mean Frank bought those?"

"Of course." Mrs Rothwell turned towards the sideboard, searching for something. "There's a card somewhere. I thought I'd taken it upstairs. I meant to, on my next trip, but you came down. Here it is!"

She handed her daughter a little envelope and Bernice gasped when she saw the name of the florist embossed in gilt on the front. But, pulling out the card and reading the message, she didn't know whether to laugh or cry. Instead, seeing the number of roses, she settled on being angry.

"Did Frank bring them? He didn't go to the expense of having them delivered, did he?"

MRS ROTHWELL watched her daughter warily, warned by the coolness of her tone.

"No, he brought them. Would it have mattered so much if he had paid for them to be delivered? That's what's troubling you, isn't it?"

"That, and the fact that he'd be so stupid as to spend all that money anyway. I'm not dying, for heaven's sake!"

"But you were happy about them, when you thought I'd bought them?"

"That was different! I don't mean I didn't appreciate what they'd cost, Mum, you know that . . ." Mrs Rothwell waved this aside ". . . but we're supposed to be saving up. We need our money!" She paused.

"It was lovely of Frank to think about sending me flowers, but a small bunch of daffs would have been just as nice, and not half as expensive. Roses, at this time of year! I ask you!"

"Perhaps he'd heard the song," Mrs Rothwell said quietly.

"Oh, I know you think I'm being horrid and ungrateful, but I want everything to be perfect when we get married. I want the house we've put a deposit on, and nice furniture, and all the things you had to do without. I don't want to have to struggle, as you did. Is that so wrong, so selfish? It's for Frank, too."

MRS ROTHWELL settled on to a stool, her eyes thoughtful and, after a moment, Bernice said:

"You don't agree. You think I'm saying I was unhappy when I was young, because sometimes I couldn't have what some girls had, but I wasn't. I'm not." She took her mother's hands between hers. "Believe me, Mum, I'm not. You and Dad gave us a childhood well worth remembering."

"I believe you. I wasn't really thinking along those lines, anyway. I was remembering when Carol and Alan were small. Did you ever wonder why there was such a gap between Alan and you?"

"I just thought . . . well, money was tight, wasn't it? Every penny had to be counted."

Mrs Rothwell grinned. "You thought we'd been practical and decided to wait until we felt we could afford another baby, didn't you? I suppose that was what we should have done, but your dad and I loved each other, and the children we already had. We simply wanted another baby.

"We weren't to be lucky, however, not right away. Then, when Alan

A Cambridgeshire Fen

THIS I remember,
    I cannot tell why,
A Cambridgeshire fen,
    And a jade-coloured sky;
Wild geese that flew
    Just as daylight was done,
White feathers gold-tipped
    By the fast-fading sun;
A frail heron perched
    On the bank of the dyke,
Patiently, hopefully,
    Waiting for pike;
A horse plodding homeward,
    An old ruined mill,
An uncanny feeling
    Of time standing still.
It's framed in my memory,
    I wish I knew why,
The silence, the stillness,
    The jade-coloured sky . . .

            Kathleen O'Farrell.

12

was six, I found I was pregnant. We were over the moon, but I miscarried. Luckily I wasn't really ill, although, of course, I was bitterly disappointed. .

"The children were too young to understand, they only knew that Mummy was sick and had to stay in bed for a few days. But it was the Sunday school outing — remember them?" Mrs Rothwell asked.

Bernice nodded vigorously, her eyes lighting up with remembered excitement.

"Well, I'd always gone with them before. There were the teachers, of course, but they always needed some help and I enjoyed doing it. This time I couldn't so Dad packed their sandwiches and we gave them some spending money. They set off for Sunday school with instructions to behave themselves, and . . . can you guess what else?"

Bernice laughed. "Of course! The emergency fund. Extra money, not to be spent unless it was on something that everyone else was doing, or in an emergency. 'And I'll want to know exactly where it went,' " Bernice quoted, with a sly look at her mother.

"Did they spend it?" she asked, as her mother stayed silent.

"No-o. It wasn't that. It rained, or started to, and the trip was cancelled. Half an hour after they'd left the house they were back, complete with their carrier bags of food and plastic macs — and a large box of chocolates for 'poorly Mummy'!"

"That was sweet of them!" Bernice exclaimed. "Who would have dreamed they would have been so thoughtful?"

Mrs Rothwell said nothing. She didn't agree or disagree and Bernice guessed the next part of the story was what mattered. She waited expectantly.

"The trip was only postponed, Bernice. Next week they were to go again — but they'd spent the money we'd given them."

Bernice frowned. "It was only a few shillings, wasn't it? And they'd spent it on you?"

"Yes, it was only a few shillings, but, next week, I had to find those few shillings again. I couldn't tell two children that they'd been wrong to buy chocolates for me, could I?"

"Of course not! They'd done it because they loved you!" Bernice's voice was indignant. "You've always said that's what matters. That . . ." Her voice tailed away and she hung her head.

AFTER a few moments Mrs Rothwell got to her feet. "I think I'll make a cup of coffee. How about you? Could you drink one?"

"Mm! Yes, I'd love one. But first, there's something I've got to do," she said, getting to her feet.

"I'll go and make the coffee," Mrs Rothwell said as Bernice reached for the telephone.

"Frank," she heard her daughter say. "Frank, I do love you. I got your flowers and I just want to say . . ."

Mrs Rothwell closed the door quietly. She thought she knew what Bernice might be saying, and it was no business of hers. But she didn't think she'd make that coffee just yet. Not for a little while. □

A RCHIE MENZIES rose early from his heather bed, dipped his face in the chill water of the burn before turning his attention to breakfast. Mrs Weir at Braeside Farm had provided the eggs as payment for the odd jobs Archie had done for her last evening. Now they were sizzling in the pan, enough to satisfy an appetite sharpened by pure mountain air.

While he ate, the sun was lifting over the mountain tops filling the corries with liquid gold. Archie sighed. Despite all his years on the road, sunrise never failed to thrill him.

He'd seen many on his travels, from the wildness of Cape Wrath to the rolling border hills. There was no part of his beloved Scotland Archie hadn't visited, and he had friends everywhere.

Many an isolated cottage had Archie to thank for chopping its winter fuel; hoisting bales of straw on to a stack was child's play to him. He was a big man in heart and stature. A man at peace with himself and his lot.

THICKER THAN WATER

by IAN WILSON

A furrow creased his weather-beaten brows. It was happening quite a lot these days. And the gold signet ring on his finger with the entwined initials A.M. and K.M. was receiving more than the occasional glance.

The time had come to make a decision. For the last seventeen years, he'd been carefully avoiding Ardmore and Glen Markie, because of his past. Can I face it now, Archie asked himself?

Just lately he'd been feeling a subtle difference, a weariness after all his years on the road. That next range of hills seemed further away than before, and his bones ached from too many nights in the open air. He was getting older, he couldn't go on leading this life forever.

Uncertain of the future, he'd been thinking more and more of Alison, the daughter he hadn't seen since she was a baby.

Archie strode the path to the lofty summit of Ben Cruin, and gazed down on tiny Ardmore far below. He'd honoured his side of the bargain keeping away from Alison all those years. But his guilt had never lessened, which was why he'd never stayed in one place long.

She'd be grown up now. He desperately wanted to see her, to explain. If she'd listen . . .

He sighed. Even if there was pain in it for him, or maybe even rejection, he had to satisfy himself that Alison was all right.

He made his way down the side of the mountain to the wooded beauty of Glen Markie.

At first the river was inaccessible, visible from high above through the trees, then quite suddenly, the path dropped dramatically to the water's edge. The trees receded, forming a sunlit amphitheatre of grassy banks and outcrops of rock jutting into the river. A series of waterfalls, quiet now but furious in spate, gave the beauty spot its name, the Witches' Cauldron.

Archie clambered to the flat top of Signal Rock to take in the sweeping view. His mind was full of conflicting emotions; nothing had changed, the poignant memories still weighed heavily on his heart. This was the cost of coming back.

15

He lay down on his back in the warm sunshine. The blue vault of the sky was like some giant blank screen to project his thoughts on, and there were plenty of them.

Across the river, a young school teacher was playing games with her class of children. Their shouts and laughter seemed like an echo of his own youth all those years ago.

They'd called him "that devil, Archie Menzies," and said, "Nae guid'll come of that laddie." But there was no bad in him, more a sense of challenge and adventure which often saw him pitting his wits against Angus Crichton, the gamekeeper on Glen Markie Estate.

What battles they'd had! Many a time Archie had escaped with a fine fat trout, with Angus in hot pursuit. Other times he was caught, but there was no malice even then. Angus enjoyed the challenge of the chase as much as Archie did. The man and the boy respected each other's skills, and by the time Archie had grown up, they were firm friends.

THEN Kay Reid came into his life.
Archie was on his way home after a day in the hills, and had stopped to quench his thirst here at the Cauldron. A large stone thumping into the water nearby soaked him.

There was laughter, followed by the shout of, "Bull's eye!"

Archie shot to his feet, determined to avenge the indignity. His long legs took him to the top of Signal Rock. "Now we'll see if you're as cheeky face to face," he challenged.

His loss of face was worse when he saw who his assailant was. A young woman . . .

"I've a good mind to put you over my knee," an aggrieved Archie muttered.

"Then what are you waiting for?" She was mocking, challenging him.

Archie's heartbeat had quickened. This was no ordinary young woman facing up to him. She was quite the loveliest he'd ever seen, dark haired with a wildness in her eyes which matched his own.

The young woman dodged past him, But Archie's long arm reached out and held her fast. She struggled furiously. "Let me go, you great brute!"

Archie roared with laugher. "My but you're the fiery one. Now, I'm a peaceable man, so if you calm down I'll let you go, but only if you promise to behave yourself."

"I promise." She rubbed her arm. "That hurt."

"Serves you right. Now you've some explaining to do."

"The other girls in Ardmore have been telling me things about you."

"What things?"

"That the great Archie Menzies is not to be tamed by any woman."

Archie grinned. "Ay, I said that."

"I was curious. I wanted to find out what you were like. I dropped the stone so that you would notice me."

Archie smiled. "Och, you must be desperate if you have to find yourself a man that way." He looked the girl up and down. "No wonder — you're pretty skinny and uninteresting."

Her eyes flamed with rage. "I hate you, Archie Menzies! You'll apologise for that!" She beat ineffectually at his chest with her tiny fists. Archie laughed and pleaded surrender.

"All right, all right, I apologise! You're a beautiful young lassie."

He pulled her into the circle of his arms and kissed her soundly. "I've said I'm sorry once." He feigned surprise. "Now I'll have to do it again. I kissed you without asking your name."

"Kay Reid," she stormed, as she walked away, his laughter following her. "That's the last time you'll ever kiss me, Archie Menzies."

But Kay had already accepted the challenge. Their romance was wild and passionate, loving each other one minute, hating the next. Those with experience of these things in Ardmore shook their heads and said it would never last.

They were wrong. It seemed that at last Archie Menzies had met the woman in his life who could tame him.

Archie and Kay married and, their daughter, Alison, was born a year later.

But Archie's restlessness was soon back. He felt trapped behind the four walls of domesticity. Perhaps, it was like poaching, the thrill of the chase was more fun than the capture. The wild magic had gone from their lives.

RATHER than stay together and see their love destroyed completely, they decided to part when Alison was several months old.

"I thought I was the woman for you, Archie, but I was wrong," Kay lamented. "God go with you. I'll love you as long as I live."

They paused, and were silent for a moment, as if to slip into each other's arms one last time. Kay's eyes met Archie's and she had to bite her lips to stay silent. Then, not wishing to prolong the agony of parting, they turned away from each other and Archie slipped out into the gloaming of a summer evening.

Homework

WE'VE got to write a poem," she said,
"For English homework, Mum."
And then, for half an hour she sat
    And frowned, and bit her thumb.
"I simply don't know *what* to write."
    She sighed. "It's hard for me,
Instead of thinking lovely thoughts,
    I'd sooner climb a tree.
The singing, dancing summertime
    Is full of little wings.
I want to run and shout outdoors,
    With all the happy things.
Perhaps I'll write one by and by,
    But now, I'm off to play,"
She said, and pen and dog-eared
    book
    Were swiftly stowed away.
"I'll never be a girl for poems,"
    She cried, with real regret.
And under cloudy, golden hair
    Grey eyes looked sad — and yet,
As off she skipped, on slender legs,
    She was, in very truth,
Herself a singing, dancing poem,
    A poem entitled "Youth."
                    Kathleen O'Farrell.

For a while they wrote to each other and he sent money he made from odd jobs he did, but it was always returned. Kay obviously wanted no reminder of him. Gradually the letters ceased too.

Five years later he was back in Ardmore for Kay's funeral. Her sudden death left Archie full of guilt, and he wanted to return to bring up Alison.

His older sister, Belle, scoffed at the idea. "What nonsense, Archie! Oh yes, you could set up a home for Alison all right, but for how long? Who's going to take care of her when you get itchy feet again?"

"She's all I've got now that Kay's dead," Archie said helplessly. "What else can I do?"

Bella glanced knowingly at her husband, Neil. "We'll raise Alison as one of our own."

Archie was astonished. "But you've three boys and two girls already."

"Then she'll even up the family. There's plenty room here at Netherton Farm."

Archie was overwhelmed. Then Neil tempered his delight with their condition.

"We suggest you keep away from Alison while she's growing up."

"That's hard to take on top of losing Kay," a chastened Archie said.

"It's a question of divided loyalties," Neil replied firmly.

Archie didn't argue, but it pained him deeply. For the second time he was sacrificing happiness for love.

On his way from Ardmore, he paused once more at the Witches' Cauldron. Tears flowed down his cheeks as he gazed at the moonlit waters and thought of his courting days with Kay. It was as if all that was dearest was being washed from his life. Deep down he'd always clung to his family, and now he'd lost all of it.

After The Rain

B EADS on the clothes-line,
    Pools on the path,
Sparrows in puddles,
    Taking a bath.
Pearls upon petals,
    Gems in the grass,
Shaft of sunlight
    Glistening on glass.
Drips on the window-sill,
    Drops on the pane,
Jewelled cobwebs —
    After the rain.

Beatrice Huntingdon.

ALISON returned to the grassy bank and gathered the children round her. As she warned them that no-one was to move away from the play area, she glanced anxiously at Signal Rock. She was relieved that the big, shaggy-looking man had gone. He'd looked wild and rather frightening . . .

Maybe it's just my mood, she thought. Even the beauty of the glen seemed dulled, as if it was a symbol of all that was wrong in her life.

Until recently, life had looked promising. College graduation, working at home in Ardmore, resuming her romance with Tom Crichton. How exciting it had been making up for those years she'd been absent.

Then Tom proposed and Alison felt a chill of fear. When she said no, Tom was more bewildered than hurt.

"What's wrong, Alison?" he asked. "Is there anything I can do?"

"I'm sorry, Tom. I just need more time that's all."

"All right. I'll wait. After all, we'll have a whole lifetime together." He took her in his arms. "But I'd still like to know if there's anything worrying you?"

If Tom had made a scene about her saying no, Alison would probably have withdrawn into herself. It was his very kindness and understanding which made her confess her inner fears.

"Oh Tom, I keep thinking of Mum and Dad. If two people so dear to each other can lose their happiness, couldn't it happen to us, too? I want to wait and be absolutely certain."

Since then, Tom had been so patient, and Alison loved him all the more for it.

Alison wished the class outing had been anywhere else but near the Witches' Cauldron. There were so many sad thoughts here.

How often had she come here with Mum? They would sit on Signal Rock and talk about her father.

"Some boys in my class say Dad was a bad man because he ran away from home when I was a baby. Is that true, Mum?"

"No, dear. Your dad was a fine, wonderful man, and he didn't run away. Sometimes people can still love each other and not be happy together as husband and wife. Dad and I were like that."

Kay had enfolded the child in her arms. "Dad was rather like a wild bird. He was always restless, wanting to fly somewhere else. Wild birds can't be caged, darling, they have to be free."

"Where is Dad now?"

"Somewhere in the mountains." Kay had tried to smile but even to a child it was obvious she was trying to hide her anguish.

"Will he come back?"

"Maybe one day." She paused. "Alison — I want you to promise me something. You'll hear lots of unkind things said about Archie Menzies as you grow up. None of them will be true, so you must stick up for him."

Not long after Alison had made that promise, her mother had died unexpectedly. All through the years Sheila had kept to her bargain. Now, as she became more frustrated by her inability to commit herself fully to Tom, she blamed her inner fears on Archie. She found herself questioning her loyalty to a man who could leave his daughter and wife.

Her daydreaming was broken by one of the children. "Please, Miss Ritchie, Jimmy Steven's not here."

Alison sighed. Of all the boys likely to disobey her he was the one. Always in trouble, but nothing bad in him, just a real "laddie." She didn't panic but decided to wait for a few minutes to see if he turned up.

C AN you help me, mister? I'm stuck!"
   Archie looked up. "Now, here's something new. I never knew boys grew in trees!"

The lad had crawled out on a branch overhanging the river, and now the branch was bending ominously. It was no bother for someone of Archie's height to pluck the boy into his arms.

"I suppose you're from those children by the Witches' Cauldron?"

"Yes, mister."

"Ay, I thought so. Didn't she tell you not to wander off?"

"Yes."

"What's your name?"

"Jimmy Steven."

Archie smiled. "Well then, Jimmy Steven, you'd better go back and face the music. Off you go now."

Jimmy hesitated. "Couldn't you come back with me?"

"What for?"

"The teacher will be cross. If you told her you'd saved my life she might feel sorry for me and not give me a telling off."

Archie roared with laughter. "You've a right glib tongue, Jimmy! You'll go a long way. All right, I'll come with you. Up on my shoulders now."

Jimmy gasped. "Gosh, mister, you're tall."

"Six foot six inches. It's grand for rescuing boys from trees. There's only one disadvantage, they can't find a bed long enough for me."

Jimmy laughed and Archie knew his fright had passed.

THE suspicion in the young teacher's eyes quickly softened when she heard the story.

She smiled up at Archie. "Jimmy can be tiresome at times. I appreciate your help." As she shook hands, her own small one lingered in Archie's for a moment before being withdrawn.

Archie stared at the girl. With the breeze tugging at her hair like that, she had a familiar look that tugged at his heartstrings. She looked so like Kay . . .

He felt a storm of emotion sweeping through him, as his last, lingering doubts were swept away. The silver locket and chain she wore round her neck had been his present to Kay on their engagement.

For a moment Archie was tempted to reveal his identity. The words were already rising in his throat . . .

"Yes," Alison prompted him.

"I was glad to be of help," Archie stammered. "Goodbye," he added as he walked away.

At that moment, he felt more alienated from her than he'd ever done before, and there was nothing he could do about it. He could see how settled her life was now; there was no way he could intrude without upsetting everyone.

He felt a certain pride. Alison was a lovely girl, Belle and Alec had done a fine job raising her.

Suddenly Archie felt all those doubts he'd been suffering from vanish. I'm a man of the countryside, he thought. A rolling stone . . . I know no other way of life . . . there's plenty mileage in me yet. He was astonished he'd even considered the possibility of giving it all up!

As he set his sights on the next range of hills, Archie was whistling again, something he hadn't done for weeks.

He stopped in mid tune. His mouth still shaped for whistling widened into a mischievous grin. Suddenly he was ravenously hungry, and wasn't it strange that he was just by the boundary fence of the Glen Markie estate?

Archie chuckled, as he slipped through the fence. Surely Angus Crichton wouldn't mind an old friend having a trout for his tea?

Archie knew the river like the back of his hand. The Black Pool was deep and inviting and usually crowded with fish . . .

A RCHIE felt a stir of excitement as a plump silver trout shimmered under the surface. "Man, you're a beauty," he whispered, glancing round anxiously. He was out in the open, fishing in the laird's favourite pool.

Archie grinned in triumph as he wrapped the trout in some paper from his haversack. I'll eat well tonight, he thought.

Instinct made him turn and run when he heard the twig cracking behind him. But the wings he'd had on his heels in the distant past had deserted him and his pursuer wouldn't give up.

Breathlessly Archie turned to face his captor, a stocky, ginger-haired young man. "You've caught me fair and square." He gasped.

So You Think You Know About Ireland?

1. Which castle was set on fire by its owner rather than shelter William of Orange?
2. Which castle was the stronghold of "Silken Thomas" Fitzgerald?
3. Which castle was built by Richard de Burgh, the "Red Earl" of Ulster?

Answers below.

3. *Ballymote.*
2. *Maynooth Castle.*
1. *Athlumney Castle.*

"Now you have your fish back, you wouldn't consider letting me go?" Archie asked as he handed over the trout.

"I'm taking you in. Perhaps it'll stop you poaching again," the young gamekeeper said. "Poaching's big business these days, and you people must be made an example of."

Archie grinned. "A worthy sentiment, young man, but I'm hardly 'big business.' I only took one small trout."

For a moment, the young man's eyes wavered, then his determination returned. "Let's go."

"How is Angus Crichton these days?"

"You know him?"

21

"From 'way back. It must be many years, though, since I've seen him."

"Then, he'll be delighted I've caught one of his old enemies."

Archie smiled inwardly. "Enemy" was hardly the right word. It was Angus Crichton who had made Kay stop Archie's poaching activities — so he could have a bit of peace, he'd told her. She had, too. Archie had never poached after that.

ARCHIE'S chagrin at being caught so easily was fast disappearing as they approached the Crichtons' cottage. He was actually looking forward to meeting Angus again after so many years.

"Who's this, Tom?" Angus looked questioningly up at Archie.

"Another poacher, I caught him at the Black Pool."

"Any trouble?"

"No."

"Good lad," Angus approved. "Go and phone the police."

Archie grinned. "All right, I'll take my punishment like a man. But before you haul me off, I want you to know something, Angus Crichton. My pride's hurt that you don't recognise me!"

"Archie Menzies!" Angus exclaimed. "You left the district years ago."

"Well, I'm back, and not of my own choosing either." He stole a meaningful look at Tom.

"Fancy you being caught, Archie." Angus was amused.

"Combination of carelessness and advancing years, Angus."

"Then it won't ease your pride to know who caught you. Tom's my son."

"I might have known. Only a Crichton could have done it! You've taught him well."

"And, Tom," Angus went on, "I'd like you to meet my old great friend, Archie Menzies." His mouth broke into a sly grin. "Not every gamekeeper can say he's had the privilege of arresting his future father-in-law."

"Who'd have believed it." Archie was stunned. "A gamekeeper for a son-in-law. I'll never live this down."

Archie winked at Angus, a gesture which didn't go unnoticed by young Tom. His face clouded.

"Don't worry, Mr Menzies. If Alison can't make up her mind soon there'll be no wedding at all." He turned on his heel and walked away.

"What's wrong with the laddie?" Archie asked. "I only meant it as a joke."

"Not your fault," Angus explained. "You touched him on a raw nerve.

"Alison and he are having some difficulties at the moment. I'm not sure what — Tom won't talk about it. But I dare say they'll sort everything out, they're a good match for each other."

Archie smiled his pleasure. "Fancy that, now — your Tom and my Alison. I'm very pleased."

"Meg and I are, too."

"And where is the lady of the house?"

"Shopping. She'll be back later. She'll probably be on the next bus."

Angus punched his old friend good naturedly on the shoulder. "Fancy you being caught by my Tom."

"He's a good lad, Angus. Keen as mustard. I tried to talk him out of bringing me in but there was nothing doing."

Angus's eyes twinkled. "What about this trout? Was it worth being caught for? Let's have a look."

Archie unwrapped it, and the gamekeeper laughed uproariously. "Heavens above, man, the laird's been after this monster for weeks! Now you walk right in and poach it from under his nose!

"Tell you what, for old time's sake, I'll turn a blind eye to this one. Blame some anonymous poacher we didn't catch. We'll give it to the laird for his supper and say it was dropped during the chase."

The two old friends enjoyed the joke. There was no mistaking their delight in renewing their friendship.

"And what's brought you back to Ardmore, Archie?"

"My conscience. I thought I'd learned to live with it, but as I get older, I find I'm looking back over my shoulder more. Guilt's a terrible burden to carry, Angus. I just had to find out if Alison was all right."

Archie explained about their accidental meeting. "Alison didn't recognise me, but I'm satisfied now. She's grown into a fine young woman." He chuckled. "She's a bit of fire in her, just like Kay."

"Will you promise me that Alison never finds out about my visit, Angus? I don't want her life disturbed. Could you ask Tom not to mention it?"

"Your secret's safe, I promise. Now, you'll stay for a meal, won't you? Meg'll be home soon."

"Thanks, Angus, but I want to get myself into the hills before sunset. I've had enough of civilisation for one day."

They shook hands warmly. "Good luck, Archie."

As he strode away Archie turned to wave and called back, "Pity about that trout, though, he was a real beauty. Now I'll have to find something else for my supper."

"Not on my beat you won't!" Angus called, and Archie's booming laugh drifted back to him on the warm evening air.

THE mood was different standing by Kay's grave in the tiny cemetery overlooking Ardmore. A storm of emotion swept through Archie and he felt lonelier than at any time during all his years on the road. Had it all been worth it?

"Please forgive me, Kay," he whispered before turning his back on Ardmore for ever and took the path towards the hills.

The sun was lower now, the Witches' Cauldron in partial shadow. The children had long gone, only the silence of evening remained, a tranquil stillness.

A mocking voice drifted towards him on the evening air. "That's right, Archie Menzies. Run away again."

Someone was standing on Signal Rock silhouetted against the skyline. "Who's that?"

"You may well ask," came the reply. "Why don't you come up here and meet me face to face? Or are you scared?"

There was a hint of challenge in the voice, something Archie couldn't resist. "I've never been scared of anything in my life," he called out.

"Except responsibility for your wife and daughter."

The directness of the attack took Archie by surprise. Quickly he clambered on to Signal Rock.

"I know who you are. I recognise your voice now. This afternoon, wasn't it, with the school outing?"

"I'm surprised you remember me," the young teacher said bitterly. "You haven't done for twenty-two years."

ARCHIE faced his daughter. This was no self-composed young schoolteacher. Alison's eyes were wild and angry as she stood, feet apart, hands on hips. Just as Kay used to do when she defied him . . .

How did she recognise me, Archie wondered. How did she know I was leaving by the Cauldron?

"You're wrong, lass." Her remarks had stung Archie, but he remained calm. "I've remembered you. I've carried my guilt each waking minute of every day."

"I'm glad you've suffered," she stormed, adding scornfully, "I've always wanted to meet the man my mother said I had to be loyal to. A *fine* man, she said. Perhaps you can tell me what's so fine about walking out on your wife and daughter?"

"You make it sound so simple, Alison. It wasn't like that at all."

"Then tell me how it was! You owe me that at least."

Archie hesitated. He was reluctant to relive the past, yet he knew it was the moment to put things right. He could only hope Alison would

Tomorrow's Promise

REMEMBER when the bracken and the fern had burned away,
The lovely foliage they bore, so scorched on that sad day?
But in the course of time that passed, a miracle appeared,
One tiny, tender shoot of green the flames had left unseared.
And from that tiny, fragile stalk, which found itself alive,
Abundant spears of greenery by sun and rain did thrive.
Till overnight it seemed, that blackened patch was there no more,
The ferns had blossomed out again, but stronger than before!
And so a message is received, whate'er your darkest hour —
Take courage, friends, and in your need, new hopes arise and flower.

Elizabeth Gozney.

accept his explanation. If she didn't, he would lose her for ever.

He told her of his deep love for Kay. A love which became so destructive that they couldn't stay together any more, and so had made the mutual decision to part. It was a decision he had to live with.

"When Neil and Belle took you into their family after Kay died, I didn't want to interfere in your life," he added in a voice choked with emotion. "I wanted you to have a secure background. If I had visited you, that would have had an unsettling effect on you. I'd do anything to make up for the last years."

Alison was scornful. "Easy to say that now, but you never had to listen to Mum crying herself to sleep at night. I was only a little girl, but I can remember that."

"Stop it!" Archie shouted. "How many nights d'you think I've cried myself to sleep? What right have you to condemn me? Or am I a scapegoat because you can't make up your mind about marrying Tom Crichton?"

Alison's head jerked up in surprise. "You know about me and Tom. Who told you?"

Archie explained, then added: "What's wrong between you? He seems a fine young man."

Alison told him. She was quieter now, almost restrained. "Tom's so patient with me. But I'm so worried that I might have inherited your wanderlust. What if we get married and I can't settle down? Apart from training to be a teacher, the only world I've ever known is Ardmore. I'm content with it at the moment, but what if I develop itchy feet? Tom deserves better than that, or rather, I don't deserve him."

"I'm sorry, Alison." Archie sighed. "The last thing I want to do is to come between you and Tom. I can understand why you're scared to commit yourself, but you mustn't compare yourself and Tom with Kay and me. We are all different people and love can never be the same.

"Take your happiness while you can. Kay and I did. The time we had together was the most wonderful of my life."

"Oh, Dad!" Alison exclaimed, throwing herself into his arms. Hot tears overflowed down her cheeks as she sobbed bitterly.

Archie soothed her gently until she'd quietened again. "There now, is that better?"

He sat down and pulled her down beside him, an arm round her shoulders. Father and daughter sat in the evening stillness, each savouring the bond between them, the bond which until now had never had the chance to develop.

E VENTUALLY Alison turned and gave her father a wry smile. "I wanted to hate you, Archie Menzies, but the moment I met you this afternoon, I knew I couldn't.

"Suddenly, everything Mum had ever told me about you came flooding back. She spoke about you often and she used to sit and re-read your letters — she kept them all, you know."

Archie swallowed the lump in his throat.

"How did you recognise me?"

"When we shook hands, I saw your signet ring. Mum often talked about it. She said you'd never forget her as long as you were wearing it."

Tears came into his eyes. "Can you ever forgive me, Alison?"

"What for?" She smiled. "The important thing is that we're back together again."

"How did you know I was here at the Witches' Cauldron?" Archie asked.

"I'd been visiting Mum's grave. I saw you arriving. I guessed you'd be leaving Ardmore this way."

Archie chuckled. "That was quite a going over you gave me."

"I know, I even surprised myself," his daughter said with a smile.

"Your Tom seemed a mite put out with me. I think I should have a word with him, just to let him know there's no hard feelings about my daughter marrying a gamekeeper," he added with a grin. "Let's go back, shall we?"

"Well, this is something different." Alison laughed up at him. "Archie Menzies is actually turning his back on the open road!"

"Well, it seems to me that now I've met my family again, I ought to give them the benefit of my wisdom — such as it is."

"I suppose you'll be telling me next that your wandering days are over?"

"Not yet awhile," Archie replied. "I'm still restless, but I promise I'll be back often. I've got roots now."

"You'd better mean it, Archie Menzies," Alison flared. "Because I'm going to keep you to that promise. Mum once said that no woman could ever tame you — but I've decided to prove her wrong and to be the one to do it!"

Archie gazed lovingly at the young woman standing defiantly before him. He felt as if this was the moment he'd been waiting on for seventeen years since Kay died. "Well, Alison Menzies —" he said "— or Crichton or whatever your name is, I think you could be right."

The lowering sun peeped through the trees, tinting all it touched with gold. It smiled on the two figures momentarily blended into one as father kissed daughter in reconciliation.

"Let's go home, Dad," Alison said. □

DIABAIG

Clinging to the shores of Loch Torridon, Diabaig is a tiny village in Wester Ross. The visitor approaches it by a road from Torridon which twists and turns under the heights of Liathach and Ben Alligin. This road, while not as testing as the Bealach na Ba in Applecross, has more than its share of gradients and hairpin bends. The village itself, which boasts an Upper Diabaig and a Lower Diabaig, with its whitewashed cottages, looks out to the tip of the Applecross peninsula and the north-east coast of Skye. The road ends at Diabaig, but determined walkers can continue for about three miles to Craig, a very isolated Youth Hostel.

DIABAIG, WESTER ROSS

IT was Lewis Carter who told him, behind the mobile classroom one
dinner-break — Lewis Carter, the burster of bubbles, the spoiler of
dreams. Tim didn't believe him, of course, and said so, whereupon
Lewis Carter laughed.

"Ask your sister, then," he jeered, but Tim was reluctant to do such a
thing. Newly promoted to the ranks of juniors, Kate was scornful
nowadays of infants such as he.

Lewis Carter's secret lay heavily on Tim for several days until he
could bear it no longer. There was no-one to ask but Kate.

A TIME FOR TRUST

by
Ruth Harris

"Lewis Carter's talking rubbish," Kate said, but she hesitated, eyes flickering, so that Tim knew she was lying. Lewis Carter had been right.

"But if there isn't . . . who fills our stockings?"

"Who do you think?"

"Not . . . ?"

"Of course, stupid," Kate said.

Tim considered this extraordinary discovery, lying awake long after Mother had kissed them both good night and gone back downstairs.

"It doesn't seem fair," he whispered to Kate. "I mean there are lots of presents in a stocking and they already give us . . ."

"Of course it's fair," said Kate, who had always accepted life and everything it had to offer without question. "It's the sort of thing you have to do when you have children."

Tim watched the pale flame of the nightlight as it flickered in its glass cage, and thought about Christmas presents. Last Christmas he had given his parents a picture of Paddington Bear painted by himself, with a calendar glued slightly askew on to Paddington's suitcase. It still hung in the kitchen although by now only the month of December remained.

He remembered his last year's stocking — so full that it had slipped off the bed on to the floor. It had landed with a frightening, rustling

29

thump, waking him at four o'clock — even earlier than usual — on Christmas morning. And as if the stocking had not been enough, there had been a bicycle, too, complete with stabilisers, waiting under sheets of wrapping paper in the hall downstairs. One present from him in return for all that seemed dreadfully mean.

Tim watched his father at breakfast next morning as he glanced quickly through the newspaper before rushing off to catch his train; then at his mother carrying dishes to the sink. What presents were they planning to buy him this year?

"Do hurry up," his mother said. "We'll be late for school if you don't get a move on."

The Blackbird

I HEARD a single blackbird
　At the breaking of the dawn.
I heard him trill his first brave notes,
　As morning was reborn.
Though day was but a gentle thought,
　stirring in the night,
His first sweet notes, though hesitant,
　Proclaimed the morning light.
I listened to the melody
　He urged the world to share,
And one by one a chorus grew
　To swell the morning air.
I heard him filled with hope and joy,
　Full throated, sweet and strong.
And waking to another day —
　I thanked him for his song.

Sylvia Mountain.

"I'm not very hungry," he said. Perhaps he should ask for extra pocket money so that he could buy them another present. That didn't seem quite right either, though.

THE solution to his problem came, like an inspiration from the angels, during a rehearsal for the Nativity play. He waited until he and Kate were watching "Blue Peter" while their mother prepared the tea in the kitchen.

"Why don't *we* give *them* stockings?" he said. "That would be fair."

Kate's eyes gleamed. She loved all secrets, any kind of plot, and could turn even an expedition to the corner shop into a conspiracy. Besides, she was an organiser — the child every teacher called upon when needing something to be done.

"What a great idea!" said Kate. "Now, we must make a list. Get me a pencil and some paper. Quick!"

Oh, to be as clever as his practical sister! Kate had all the ideas; Tim carried them out. It was Kate who suggested that Tim should knock over the tins of baked beans in the supermarket so that she could buy the nuts unnoticed while Mother, red faced and apologetic, rebuilt the pyramid. It was Kate who organised their secret expedition to the greengrocer to buy tangerines and the biggest coconut in the shop, and it was Kate who took charge of their pocket money and worked out what they could or could not afford.

But it was Tim who had to go into Duval's, the luxury chocolate shop next to the greengrocer. Duval's chocolates were Tim's idea.

"They *are* the best in town," he urged. "I heard Father say so."

"I'm not going in there," Kate said firmly. "You can if you want to."

So he did, clutching in his clenched fist the coins she had allotted, while she hovered on the pavement outside, peering anxiously between the trays of fruit creams, bonbons, caramels and truffles in the window, to make sure that he was all right.

The girl behind the counter looked like a doll. She had glossy maroon lips and the spiky black lashes round the wide open eyes gave her a startled expression.

"Have you got enough money?" she asked Tim suspiciously. "Mind you don't breathe on the chocolates now!"

"It's all I've got," Tim explained timidly, uncurling his fingers and showing her the coins. "Just a few will do. It's for a Christmas present."

The girl took his money and told him how many chocolates he could choose. Not many, he reflected, as he took the small paper bag. But then, they were the best.

Kate, who fancied herself as an artist, took charge of the drawing and painting. Pocket money did not run to wrapping paper, so she made their own, covering newspaper with swirls of brilliantly-coloured poster paint.

Tim did the hard work. He found the pebbles for Kate to decorate and turn into paperweights. He retrieved foreign Christmas card envelopes from the wastepaper basket and floated off the stamps in saucerfuls of water under his bed, to give to Father for his stamp collection.

They were totally preoccupied and Tim went through the days in a dream.

M ISS DAVIES rang me last night," his mother said, as the three of them walked down the hill to school one morning. "She says your mind's not on your work. You're not worried about anything, are you?"

Tim stared up at her in fright. Whatever could he say?

"Is Lewis Carter bothering you?" his mother asked.

He shook his head. He knew he mustn't lie.

"I'm thinking about Christmas," he said at last. "I'm wondering what Father Christmas is going to bring."

Beyond his mother's arm he saw Kate's anxious expression change to a sudden, appreciative grin. He felt proud that he hadn't given away their secret.

"Why don't you think about work when you're at school?" his mother suggested. "And leave Father Christmas until you come home. I'm sure that would be best."

It wasn't easy, being Father Christmas. All sorts of unexpected problems occurred. How to keep the chocolates was one. Duval's elegant pieces were no temptation; the strong scent of violets made them not very appetising for boys, Tim thought.

31

But the number of gold-wrapped chocolate coins, which had been quite a treasure trove at the beginning of December, grew rapidly less as Christmas Day approached.

Kate accused Tim — Tim accused Kate. Both knew themselves to be guilty. One chocolate bar had been visibly nibbled down one side, but Tim hoped that a mouse might be blamed for that.

Another problem was the stockings themselves. What could they put the presents into? Father's socks were much too small for Father Christmas's pile of presents.

The stockings filled by Father Christmas for Tim and Kate in previous years were not stockings at all but paper sacks, decorated with jolly Father Christmas and laughing rednosed reindeer. Neither child knew where they had come from.

In the end, a pair of tights borrowed by Kate from the airing cupboard proved more satisfactory than anyone might have imagined — one leg for Mother, one for Father and the top for joint presents.

And last of all, how were they to wake in the middle of the night?

"Suppose I drink lots of water before I go to bed?" Tim suggested.

"That wouldn't work," Kate said scornfully. "You wouldn't wake and then Mother'd be cross in the morning." She thought about his suggestion for a while. "Still, it's not a bad idea," she said at last, grudgingly. "It'll be all right if I do it."

In the past it had always seemed as if Christmas would never come. This year it was a rush to get everything ready in time — the presents made, wrapped, stowed into the tights and hiding the resulting unwieldy, two-legged bundle under Kate's bed.

"And remember," Mother said, as she kissed them good night on Christmas Eve, "to keep your eyes closed tight if you're still awake when Father Christmas comes, or he won't leave you any presents." Kate and Tim looked at each other across the gap between their beds and giggled.

"I shan't be able to get to sleep ever," Tim said, and believed it. But suddenly it was the middle of the night and Kate was shaking him awake.

He had never known the house so cold. His shadow went before him like a giant as he struggled with his half of Father Christmas's awkward bundle. How lucky, Tim thought, that he was still not sure about the wolves behind the wardrobe.

Without the nightlight even Kate would not have found her way without stumbling, and probably waking Mother and Father.

B UT their parents were already awake, lying without moving, scarcely drawing breath, terrified that their children might realise they were no longer sleeping.

After what seemed hours, the rustling stopped. So too did the childish whispers. Uncertain footsteps made their way to the door. The loose board on the landing gave one last creak.

Subdued giggles came from the children's room, tentative rustling, excited whispers.

Mother took a deep breath and sat up. "I thought they'd never go. "They've discovered their stockings," she said. "What were they doing here? For a moment I thought one of them must be ill."

Father tiptoed to the door and closed it quietly, while Mother reached for the bedside lamp. Warm, pink light flooded the room. They both stared.

"Heavens!"

"What on earth . . . ?"

AT the bottom of the bed a large poster, hanging between the bedposts, wished them "A VERY MERRY CHRISTMAS." On the bedspread beneath rested a large, unevenly - stuffed, double-tailed brown snake.

"Well!" Father said at last. "Do you think we should investigate? They never wait, after all! Let's follow their example . . . Gracious, a coconut! Do you think that's to hang from the cherry tree for the birds — or is it really for us?"

"Kate adores coconut milk," Mother said, smiling, remembering a glimpse of an unwieldy parcel being hurried upstairs by Kate and Tim and not really thinking about it at the time.

PEACE

I HAVE seen peace in sunset hues, in reflections etched on placid waters, in the face of a sleeping child, in music of slow movements.

I have also seen peace in the amber depths of a dog's eyes. Like hands holding me in their grasp.

Such the eyes of a dog at peace who dwells in the secure affection of her people — and knows it!

Lovely to behold; more rewarding to discover. Scripture has its radiant promise: "Thou wilt keep him in perfect peace whose mind is stayed on thee."

Wonderful to find peace, perfect peace, shining from the deep golden caverns of a dog's eyes. Because her life is stayed in utter confidence. In those who love her.

Rev. T. R. S. Campbell.

"That's it, then. They must have chosen the largest one in the shop. Your tights will never be the same again."

"It's a small price to pay. Whatever do you think gave them the idea? I thought Tim still believed in Father Christmas!"

"Some child at school will have disillusioned him. You know how it is — there's always someone wanting to show off how clever he is."

Smiling tremulously at each other, they pulled the little parcels out of the tights, one after another. The wrapping paper was already coming apart, revealing the contents — little packets of paper clips, peanuts and raisins, a rubber, foreign stamps curling at the edges . . .

"Now I understand the reason for those saucers of water," Mother exclaimed. "Tim said he might get thirsty during the night, and when I said, 'Rubbish,' he said he was worried about the mice behind the walls. For some odd reason he thought the water would keep them away."

C

"But they aren't . . . " Father began, suddenly sounding anxious.

"Of course not. It was just Tim trying desperately to come up with a good reason!"

"I say," said Father, "aren't these chocolates from Duval's? What made them go there, do you think? So expensive — they must have been saving up for weeks. Even so, how on earth did they manage to get the money? They must have scraped together every last penny of their pocket money, plus what remained of birthday present money from the various relatives."

"I can't stand Duval's chocolates," Mother said ruefully. "So scented. They remind me of my great-aunt Ann. She used to chew violet cachous and then breathe over me when I was a child. It made me feel sick every time."

"You'll have to force yourself to enjoy them . . . You can't let the children know you don't really like them. It looks as if someone already has enjoyed some of this chocolate," Father said, looking at it more closely.

"It must have been Tim." Mother's smile was tender. "Look, you can see the mark of his teeth, the front one so crooked. I couldn't possibly eat that. Pass me a tissue, darling, will you? I shall keep it to remind me . . ."

They surveyed their gifts again, passing them to each other and marvelling at the thought and the planning which must have taken place.

FATHER made an early-morning cup of tea. They drank it in the rosy glow of bedside lights, warming their hands on the cups and gazing at the little pile of treasures lying in front of them.

The powder of the poster paint on the wrapping paper had transferred itself from the newspaper to the bed-sheet, so that the once-white cotton was now gaily multicoloured.

"I still can't believe that they did it all by themselves," Mother said. "They must have planned for weeks . . . I never suspected a thing, you know. I would never have thought they could have kept it secret, not at their age."

"They're all right, aren't they?" Father said. "You know . . . I worry sometimes, about Tim being so timid . . ."

Mother nodded in understanding.

"And Kate so bossy . . ." she added.

There was a suspicion of tears underlying the smiles, but they were tears of happiness.

"But underneath all that . . . we're very lucky."

They both knew it. But Mother's last thought, as she slipped into sleep, was of the piece of chocolate waiting in the bedside drawer to join the other mementos of childhood.

One badly-nibbled half-square of chocolate, marked by the crooked indentation of her son's milk teeth; to be remembered and smiled over in years to come as a reminder of the visit of her own, her very own, Father Christmas. □

You Can't Beat The Human Touch

by
Ailie Scullion

"COMPUTERS, Miss MacBride, could solve most of our world's problems."

My employer, Mr Edward Roberts, was off on his favourite subject again. He waved his long thin arms about frantically as he explained how he'd designed his kitchen to take the drudgery out of housekeeping. Each gadget, he assured me, had been personally installed and would answer immediately to my demands.

"Take this microwave oven." He smiled enthusiastically. "It's the latest design and I've included sophisticated techniques for accident-free cooking. But I expecct you'll find that out for yourself when you cook our supper tonight. Now are you sure you understand everything I've been telling you?"

I smiled feebly. I would never remember half the things he'd told me — not in a million years.

On the other hand Pat MacBride was not one to admit defeat easily.

Besides, the wage Mr Roberts had mentioned was not to be scoffed at — although I was also assured I would earn every penny of it when the twins arrived home from boarding school. I suddenly remembered he added that bit with a sad shake of his head.

Ed Roberts was a scientist who worked at a nearby research institute. The folk in the domestic agency had nicknamed him their "Mad Professor." His button-controlled kitchen had been the talk of the office.

From the window, I watched him climb into a low-slung sports car then fold up his long legs to fit. I rather liked Mr Roberts, especially that endearing tuft of fair hair which refused to obey his ministrations with a wet comb.

Once on my own I wandered about his kitchen, rather tentatively pressing a button here and pulling a lever there, and watching the place galvanise into activity. Truly mind boggling — but an adventure in a culinary sort of way.

The fridge, however, took me completely by surprise. When I opened the door, a disembodied voice informed me: "Ice-cubes require renewing, please."

I JUMPED back as though I'd been stung. No wonder the agency could hardly cope with the Roberts household's demand for live-in housekeepers. It would have required a chief engineer's ticket to operate all these dials.

Since his wife died two years ago, Mr Roberts had used his particular skills and adapted his kitchen so that everything would obey his command. It was a pity he had not made allowances for the likes of myself, who had problems changing a fuse. Well, I'd just have to learn to adapt, I told myself.

I studied one label marked *Auto-kettle*. Uneasily I pressed the button and watched in utter amazement as a lid flew up and a jet of water was directed inside. The water was boiling before I'd regained my composure. My "nice cup of tea" didn't do much to restore my nerve, or my confidence.

I decided I'd better make a thorough investigation of the kitchen to see if I could find anything familiar to me.

I found the slow cooker in a cupboard under the sink. It still had a label attached to its lid which informed me that it was a "gift from Aunt Betsy."

Now slow cookers I know about. Safe as houses, and they would never dream of talking back. I prepared my favourite meat casserole complete with veg., herbs and spices, plugged it in, then went to examine the rest of the house.

The bedrooms were no less frightening. There was an intercom connecting the professor's with every other room in the house. There was also a specially-designed desk which slid across the bed and allowed the man to go on working without getting up. I'd heard of workaholics but this was ridiculous!

His study, too, had me going about on tip-toe. Books, some of which he had written himself, ranged along one wall. I opened one and tried to read it but it seemed filled with a language I'd never heard about — the language of science presumably!

There was a word processor, of course, and a telephone-answering machine. Beside them were two gilt-framed photographs — one of Mr Roberts' late wife, a small dark-haired lady, and the other of two fair-haired solemn-faced boys, identical in every feature. They bore a striking resemblance to Mr Roberts.

GEORGE and Stevie. I was supposed to meet them at the railway station at 11.05 minutes precisely.

They were coming home on holiday, my employer had announced rather defensively, and he would expect them to cause as little trouble as possible. He had, after all, taught them to be completely self-sufficient. Poor wee mites, I thought. Fancy being 10 years old and expected to be self-sufficient.

Even the Mini was automatic. I drove carefully to the station, thinking all the way about the two small boys who had been torn from their home for a

Snow-spangled

ICE-VEINED the hawthorn, frost on the bough,
 Webs of white lace thread the grass;
Chill of the moon, as its rays search the lochs,
 Splinters of silver on glass.
Flurries the wind through the starkness of trees,
 Etches of black upon white;
Whipping the skeletal left-over leaves,
 Patches of shadow and light.
Thin puffs of snowflakes spiral the scene,
 Hinting of blizzards to spread —
Winter decides on its theme for New year,
 Forecasting shivers ahead!

Elizabeth Gozney.

whole term and now their father wouldn't even be at the station to greet them. I wondered if they realised they didn't have a life like a normal family's.

As the train doors slid open, two pocket editions of Mr Roberts stepped determinedly on to the platform. They walked in step and proffered their hands at exactly the same moment. I was soon to learn they did most things in unison.

"You'll be Dad's latest . . ." announced the one with *George* printed in red across his T-shirt.

". . . live-in housekeeper," Stevie echoed.

"Looks a bit on the young side, don't you think?"

"Perhaps," the other agreed, "but she should brighten the place up a bit. Have you ever seen such red hair?"

Self-sufficient they might be, I decided, but I was not going to tolerate rudeness.

"Would you mind not discussing me when I'm present?"

They looked at me in surprise.

"Of course, Miss . . . I'm afraid we don't know what to call you."

"You can call me Pat."

"Miss Pat. We didn't realise we were offending. Dad has always taught us to discuss things openly and not behind people's backs. He says that's very rude indeed."

They smiled at me almost sympathetically as they climbed into the car.

George, I noticed, had a rather irritating cough. When I mentioned this, I was informed that it had come as the result of playing a disgusting game called rugby. "George is not very sports orientated, Miss Pat," Stevie explained.

I was also to learn that one twin invariably answered the other's questions. Like everything connected with the Professor it just added to the general confusion, but I was determined not to be beaten so early in my new job.

That night George coughed and coughed and kept everyone awake. Mr Roberts arrived at the upstairs bedroom wearing black and gold striped pyjamas and a worried expression.

"Can't we do something for him?" he suggested wearily. "Call the doctor out and get an antibiotic?"

I shook my head.

"I've taken his temperature and it's normal. The cough's just in his throat; irritating but not serious. Probably the more he tries to stifle it, the more insistent it becomes. I know what it's like — it gets to the stage where the cough tires you out. I've made him up butter-balls in sugar. That always did the trick for me when I was his age. Let's try it, anyway."

My employer looked suitably impressed but squirmed in sympathy as I slipped one inside George's mouth and waited until it slipped down. After the second treatment, the coughing subsided.

Love's Magic

WE can't define love,
It's both pleasure and pain —
Savage, yet gentle
As soft summer rain.

It's fragile, yet strong
As a deep-rooted tree —
Tender, yet wild
As a turbulent sea.

It's older than winter,
And younger than spring —
Love's a mysterious,
Magical thing.

Eileen Thomas.

THE three males of the household smiled at each other in relief.

"Remarkable, Miss MacBride," Mr Roberts complimented. "Or may I also call you . . ."

"Pat? Of course. Everyone does."

"Good then, Pat. Perhaps we could nip down to the kitchen for some hot chocolate, since we're all up anyway?"

You Can't Beat The Human Touch

So the four of us trooped down to the kitchen, late hour or not.

I left it to him to press the button which caused a saucepan of milk to rattle just before the milk came to the boil.

Mr Roberts sipped his mug of hot chocolate, then cleared his throat.

"That was a particularly fine casserole you prepared tonight, Pat. The meat was extremely tender. Would you mind writing down your recipe so I can give it to . . ."

An unexpected blush crept up Mr Roberts' face. He had been just about to say "my next housekeeper."

As the twins were despatched back to their beds Mr Roberts looked across at me hopefully.

"What do you think of my sons?"

"They're nice enough," I started cautiously, then watched him frown.

"Do I detect some reservations?"

Now Pat MacBride never believed in beating about bushes and after all the man had asked.

"Well, you must admit, Mr Roberts, that they're not like real boys. I have two young brothers and they're a pair of holy terrors; never out of hot water at school. But, you know, we prefer it that way; it seems the natural way for boys to behave. They would certainly never spend an entire afternoon fooling about with a computer in their bedroom, or discussing the possibility of cloning white mice."

"You think the twins might be too advanced for their age?" he suggested mildly.

I nodded.

He considered my point of view carefully. "You may have a point, Miss Pat, but they dislike the more . . . ahem . . . physical games. I was never too fond of them myself at school. I always seemed to have things to do which interested me more."

"But they're so pale! You must see that for yourself. I think they should get out and about more. Even if they don't take part in team games, there are plenty of other things to do outdoors."

"Do as you see fit, Miss MacBride," Mr Roberts instructed stiffly. "When Jean was alive she used to attend to such things."

With that, he tightened the cord of his dressing-gown and departed upstairs.

So it was back to Miss MacBride again. I felt as though I'd been slapped in the face, but Rome was not built in a day, I reminded myself.

NEXT morning George's cough had completely disappeared so I suggested we all went for a swim. The twins looked at me in horror.

"You mean . . . for pleasure?" George asked.

"We've never done that before," Stevie said thoughtfully.

I decided it was time to ask some questions myself in preparation for my new regime.

It turned out that at their boarding school the twins were made to attend a local swimming pool but had perfected the art of hiding in the shower rooms until it was time for the lesson to come to an end.

When I reproached their father, he looked positively downcast.

"I can see what you mean, Miss Pat, but I never learned how to swim myself. You must understand that over the years I have only taught them what I know about."

Typical, I thought. Absolutely typical!

Well, today was Saturday, I reminded him and he didn't have to go into the institute. Why didn't we all take a trip to the swimming pool and rectify this lapse in their education?

I was feeling absolutely superior by this time and informed the boys' father about the gold medal I'd won for life-saving. Then I reminded him how it was everybody's duty to at least learn how to stay afloat.

I have to admit they all looked rather comical as they stood beside the pool in their brand-new swimming trunks. Mr Roberts was shivering violently as he dipped one toe into the water.

I took the boys on first. They learned quickly and were soon splashing about excitedly as all healthy young boys should.

Mr Roberts was made of sterner stuff. His long, lean body resisted my every command, tensing every time I asked him to relax. I could see he was trying so hard to obey my instructions, but each time he raised his feet from the bottom he would sink like a stone.

It took almost an hour just to get him to float. Then, with my hand cupped under his chin, we went through the various movements. He seemed extraordinarily pleased with his progress.

Once, his cheek brushed against mine, and such a thrill passed through my body I almost let him drop. He must have felt it, too, for he gave me a strange look.

AFTER our swimming lesson a strange new harmony descended upon the Roberts household. I got Mr Roberts to remove all the "voices" from his kitchen for a start.

"After all," I suggested gently, "cooking should be a journey of imagination."

A slow smile climbed up his lean features until it reached his fine grey eyes. "I must admit I've never thought of it that way before," he confessed.

After that, he took a keen interest in the meals I prepared, enquiring about the various ingredients and flavourings — and, I was sure, not because he wanted the information for his next housekeeper!

The twins were improving, too. We'd go down to the swimming pool twice a week and they always returned home with cheeks aglow and magnificent appetites. But they had not altogether abandoned their original pursuits and still spent hours in their room with their computer.

One morning they invited me upstairs with them. They wanted to co-ordinate some experiment.

Anxious to capitalise on our new-won cameraderie, I willingly went along.

"Ask her, Stevie," George urged, his fingers poised above a keyboard.

"All right. What age are you, Miss Pat?" he demanded bluntly. "Twenty-six," I replied guardedly.

Stevie nodded approvingly. "Splendid. Splendid. Now tell me, are there any attachments? Engaged, perhaps . . . ? Spoken for . . . ?"

Such old-fashioned words for a ten-year-old! I shook my head and was immediately told to answer "yes" or "no."

"No then," I retorted too loudly. Thereupon I was bombarded with a series of the most personal questions which brought equally curt replies from me.

I was sorely tempted to refuse to answer, but I didn't want to destroy this evidence of the boys' trust in me.

At last the inquisition was complete. The boys seemed highly satisfied with their print-out and studied it carefully, their fair heads close together.

"I think she might do very nicely." George and his twin nodded sagely. "I'm just not too sure about the red hair."

"I have warned you two about discussing someone in her presence," I reminded them.

They looked suitably penitent.

"Just a habit, Miss Pat. We were thinking aloud."

"Well, think about this then," I retorted. "What about a picnic at the seaside on Sunday? I noticed a rather nice little beach from the window of the train. If the weather's good, we could leave early and make a day of it."

The twins looked at each other.

The Reawakening

THE smallest hint of joys to come can
    make a sad heart sing,
The first small bud upon a tree — a
    swallow on the wing.
The first bright hint of sunlight's gold
    that seemed so long delayed.
Heart-warming moments when no-one
    could ever feel dismayed.
The earth may still look bare and
    cold, but when first snowdrops
    peep,
We know that nature never dies, but
    only lies asleep.
Eternal life, eternal hope, forever shall
    remain,
So long as turning of the year brings
    springtime's joy again.

Georgina Hall.

"That must be Corbyhead, Miss Pat, and yes, we would love to go for a picnic. Can we ask Dad to come, too?"

I had not intended to include Mr Roberts, but they were out of the room like two flashes of greased lightning. Within minutes they were back to report that their father would be delighted to join us.

SO there we all were on this empty white beach with the waves piling one on top of the other and the twins showing off their crawl to a suitably-impressed father. Mr Roberts had found himself a flat rock to stretch out upon but I'd noticed he was sporting his swimming trunks and looked at him hopefully.

He seemed to read my thoughts, but there was a plea in his face. "Must I go in? You must know I'll never feel really at home in water."

I was inclined to agree and relented enough to join him on top of the rock.

"The twins really like you, Pat," he began immediately. "I've never heard them say so much about anyone I've employed before."

"Really?"

He nodded his head. "I've been thinking a lot about the things you said about them. Perhaps I have failed . . . filling their minds with knowledge instead of . . ."

"Love," I suggested gently.

He nodded. "When Jean was alive, the problem didn't exist. I never had much to do with the running of the home — too busy up at the institute — but Jean used to work a lot with the boys . . . the way you do. It has brought back a lot of memories."

A forlorn look passed across his face as he spoke. I wanted to take him into my arms and hug him close . . .

It was crazy! How could I possibly feel anything for a man who could only respond when a button was pressed?

"I'm going in for my swim," I told him gruffly.

Rising quickly, I ran across the sands with the echo of his voice following me. "I'll come in too . . . if you really want?"

But I wanted to be alone. Out there amongst the waves I could cool my flaring cheeks and wash away such a crazy notion.

I STRUCK out strongly away from the shore. The deeper water was tinged with green and decidedly colder. After a while I rested and trod water.

It was then I heard his cry.

"Help! Help!"

I could see him, my poor floundering professor, all arms and legs and filled with panic. He'd taken cramp when he attempted to follow me out of his depth.

The twins were on the beach shouting as I struck out back towards the splashing figure. I reached him and he was gulping for air as I turned him on to his back. Supporting his head, I towed him back.

Later, we lay exhausted on the sand. The twins were still sobbing and looking just like frightened ten-year-olds instead of the miniature Einsteins they sometimes appeared to be.

"Why?" I gasped when I recovered some breath. "Why on earth did you do that?"

"I wanted to ask you something while it was still in my mind," he said apologetically.

"Couldn't it have waited until I came ashore?" I demanded.

He just shook his head, showering me with salt water.

"All right," I said at last. "What was so important that it couldn't wait?"

"Will you marry me, Pat MacBride?"

You Can't Beat The Human Touch

HE said it just like that, with us both still fighting for breath and dripping wet.

The twins were leaning close so they could hear me reply. Ed was smiling proudly up at his sons.

"They showed me their print-out this morning, Pat. They've been carrying out an experiment — a compatibility test. I'll show it to you if you like," he offered.

What a confounded cheek, I thought. Those two little monsters running my statistics through their machine, then matching them up with their dad's!

"What was the result?" I found myself asking lamely.

Ed's long lean face lit up.

"Oh, a perfect combination. Opposites attracting and all that. Of course, I suspect these two may have doctored some of the evidence so as it would fit. But they both wanted the experiment to succeed."

I drew in a deep breath. "Do you have some sort of aversion to bright red hair?"

"None whatsoever," he replied immediately. "It reminds me of the setting sun, and your eyes . . ."

"Never mind about that," I broke in sharply. "You're telling me that you're willing to abide by the decision of some machine. Do you think that's all there is to choosing a partner?"

It was as close as that. If he had said yes I would probably have gone back and packed my bags. Instead Ed put his long arms around my wet shoulders and his cheek came to rest against mine.

"Do you think I need a computer to tell me how I feel about you, Pat? What about that day at the swimming pool? Admit it! That was pure chemistry we felt. Now tell me — will you marry me?"

I looked up, expecting the twins to move away.

Not they! They were staying where they were, with bated breath, to hear my reply.

Oh well, I told myself philosophically, one could not have everything. I moved myself into a more comfortable position within his arms and asked:

"Which button do I press for yes?" □

NEVER JUMP TO CONCLUSIONS

A NYONE who knows the small, rather remote village of Tillydrem will be aware that many customs and traditions there are ones which may be found in other places.

There is the annual firework display in November, the ploughing match in spring, the baking competition at the Woman's Guild. All these sort of things are usual enough.

But where else will you find something which is known quite simply as the "Tattie Planting Holiday"? It is held on the first Friday in May, and is now really just an old tradition which has hung on year after year, even though no longer useful as it was these many years ago.

Two or three of the older people can remember when it was a useful day, when local children went out to the surrounding farms and planted potatoes in the long drills already prepared by a plough drawn by a pair of horses.

"It was always done on the Friday afternoon," old Geordie Bryce would say nostalgically. "All the bairns worked and the job was done in no time. You got a basket or a pail, and filled it from the sacks they had left across the field. You got a wee stick, too, for measuring the right

by ANNE MURRAY

length between each tattie, then when a whole drill was planted the plough came again and turned over the earth. It was a great afternoon, and if the work wasn't finished, there was always the Saturday to do that."

Of course, for years now the potatoes have been planted in a much more modern way, by machine. There is no need for schoolchildren to have a holiday that afternoon, and officially they don't have one at all. But somehow each succeeding generation has seen to it that they do, and the way it is worked out is quite simple.

Instead of an hour's break for dinner at twelve o'clock, school keeps going for half an hour longer. Well, that is afternoon, isn't it? So there you have an afternoon attendance, even if the children are released at half past twelve!

It need hardly be said that none of them go planting potatoes, But what a lot of other things there are to do! Somehow, the fact that this holiday isn't used the way it was originally meant to be gives it a special flavour of its own, so that it is prized and treasured. Whether the authorities know about it no-one bothers to inquire, and any new teacher coming to the

45

school in Tillydrem is sure to hear about it in advance from somewhere.

At least that is what happened before the arrival of Miss Sara Milton to take charge of the small school. This time, however, there was a slip-up somewhere. Perhaps it was because the teacher she was to succeed gave up unexpectedly during the Easter holidays, and it then seemed a good idea to bring in early the successor who was engaged to start work in August.

It was when Mrs Jackson suddenly became ill that someone recalled the interview where Miss Milton revealed how she wasn't employed at the moment. Why not ask her to come right away?

S ARA MILTON was only too pleased to do that. After a year out of a settled job, doing occasional temporary work, she had been thrilled to be offered the post of teacher at Tillydrem. How wonderful it would be to exchange the crowds and bustle of a big city for the quiet and peace of the country, and how delightful to find a pleasant schoolhouse awaiting her!

She didn't mind a bit that it was a long way from any large town, nor that many things would be different. All she wanted was to work hard at her post and, in time, get the school running on the lines she favoured, probably a little more modern than at present.

And at first all went well. As Sara Milton got to know the youngsters she found them a delightful lot, much easier to handle than some of the tough city types she had encountered before. But it really was a pity·that no-one remembered to warn her about the Tattie Planting Holiday. The first she heard about it was halfway through that Friday morning when she had got the older children writing an essay, and the younger ones doing drawing.

The small ones were real pets, Sara thought, as she surveyed the orderly room. Three days a week she had the assistance of Mrs Hendry, an elderly retired teacher, who took them into another room, But this wasn't one of Mrs Hendry's days, and Sara was into the way of coping with the different ages now.

Yes, life in Tillydrem was good, she thought. She'd met quite a lot of the people now and found them friendly. The fact that there seemed few young men around didn't worry her in the least. She was much more interested in her job at present than anything in the way of romance. And that was the way it would continue, she resolved, as she saw little Maisie Thomson put up a hand.

"Yes, Maisie?" she asked kindly.

"Please, miss, can I get away five minutes early?" said Maisie. "My mummy's taking me to Dremlachie and the bus goes at half past twelve."

Sara gazed back in perplexity.

"You'll be at home having your lunch at half past twelve, Maisie," she pointed out. "I think you've made a mistake, for your mummy hasn't said anything about taking you off school this afternoon . . ."

A chorus of voices arose at that, and it was some time before she could make sense of what her pupils were saying. It was 10-year-old Brian Gillon, the minister's son, who tried to make everything clear.

"It's our Tattie Planting Holiday," he told his puzzled teacher. "We don't go for our dinners at twelve. We stay in another half-hour, then we're finished for the day. It's OK, miss, it's always this Friday."

Sara smiled. They were cunning little scamps. Fancy trying to get an extra half-holiday out of her like this!

"Nonsense!" she said briskly. "This afternoon isn't a holiday, so just get on with your work and then go for your dinner break at the usual time."

Janey Gordon, who came from one of the outlying farms, burst into tears.

"I haven't got my packed lunch with me," she wailed. "I'll have to go home, miss, or I won't have any dinner at all."

It seemed that nobody had brought food with them today, all sure they would get home for it. Sara frowned. This was ridiculous! She tried to discover more.

"Why do you think you should get a holiday today?" she demanded.

"It's for planting the tatties for the farmers," a dozen voices informed her.

"I saw fields of potatoes being planted last week," Sara countered. "It isn't done by hand nowadays."

"We could still do it if anyone wanted us," argued Brian. "And, please, miss, my uncle's coming specially from Glasgow to take me up the river to show me how to fish. I got a rod for my birthday . . ."

"Sorry, Brian, just tell your uncle to come tomorrow, then you'll have the whole day," Sara suggested.

"He can't come tomorrow, he's going to a riot," Brian declared. "At least, it's a protest march or something, and he says it'll likely be a fine riot before it ends. Oh, miss, he's coming specially!"

"So you said," Sara broke in. "Now will you please all get on with your work until twelve o'clock. Anyone who hasn't brought lunch can just stay in the school as usual and I'll see what I can find."

BUT when it was 12, and Sara dismissed them, not a child lingered. Going to look out a few minutes later, she found the playground deserted. It looked as though the country children had just set off for home.

Would any return at one o'clock? She began to feel doubtful as she went across to the schoolhouse for her own lunch. It was as she put her key into the door that she heard footsteps and turned to see Brian Gillon racing towards her.

"Miss, my uncle's here, and when I told him you didn't want us to have a holiday he laughed and said, 'Doesn't she know Tillydrem is a law unto itself?' I said you asked why he couldn't take me fishing tomorrow — and he really is going to the riot." He paused for breath. "Then he said I'd better come and tell you no-one will be at the school this afternoon, and to enjoy your holiday. Peter Munro and Bill Matheson are going up the river with us, and my little brother, Sandy, wants to come too. Cheerio, miss, see you on Monday."

"Brian, wait! Brian!" she called after him as he rushed off, but her call was in vain. This was unbelievable, she decided in annoyance. And this uncle from Glasgow seemed to be encouraging the children to defy her.

She just wished she had him here! Yes, she'd let him know it wasn't his business to come here and laugh about it all. Oh, he'd probably be one of these scruffy, weirdly-dressed types, she supposed, set on joining a protest march and ready to make trouble at it. What a brother for the Tillydrem minister to have!

There was an idea now. She'd go right along to the Manse and see what Mr Gillon thought about the holiday. He and his wife had been very nice to her, and they might well agree to stop Brian playing truant this afternoon . . .

ONLY the minister and his wife were there when Sara reached the Manse. The fishing party, it seemed, had taken lunch with them and gone off immediately.

"You didn't know about the holiday?" exclaimed Mrs Gillon in surprise. "Oh dear, someone should have told you."

The minister looked concerned.

"Folk here expect everyone to know all that goes on." He sighed. "But don't worry, Sara. Just enjoy a free afternoon, and on Monday it would probably be wiser to say nothing about it to the youngsters."

"After all, it's just an old Tillydrem custom that began long before any of them were born." Mrs Gillon smiled. "So you can't blame them."

Sara felt let down. She walked back to the schoolhouse, beginning to think Tillydrem had its drawbacks. As for that young man sending a message to her to enjoy the holiday. He had a nerve! She began to rehearse all the things she'd like to say to him, then paused as a voice spoke to her over a garden hedge.

"A grand afternoon for your holiday, Miss Milton," remarked stout Mrs Munro. "Are you off for a walk? If you take the river path maybe you'll see my Peter, for he went there with the minister's laddie."

"So I understand," Sara answered curtly. "This holiday is all nonsense!"

Another face looked over the next-door hedge. But she just gave a nod to Mrs Boyd and hurried on, leaving the two women to speculate on why Miss Milton seemed so out of temper.

When it became apparent that no children were returning in the afternoon, it was depression more than annoyance that settled on Sara. She had plainly told her pupils that they were to come back and they had all defied her. Nor had there been any help from the minister, with his advice to say nothing about it on Monday. Well, she'd see about that!

Tillydrem no longer seemed such a delightful place, even with the sun shining and the air warm for early May. Perhaps she shouldn't have accepted this post, just stayed on in the city, hoping for some suitable job to turn up. Or perhaps she should have accepted the proposal of Gerald Dawson, which he had made rather unexpectedly when he heard she was leaving.

She had known Gerald for a long time. But, no, not even when he told her he loved her could she feel anything for him but friendship, not at all the sort of deep affection which would lead to a good, solid marriage which would last.

GAZING out at the quiet playground, Sara sighed. She had never yet seen anyone who stirred her in the least, and it hadn't really worried her. Her parents had married in their late thirties, and didn't her mother often say that had been a good idea? Their marriage had certainly worked out well.

"I was thirty-seven when I married," Mrs Milton would tell people. "I'd had lots of fun, and enjoyed working till then. But after getting married I didn't need to bother about work, just enjoyed being a housewife and mother."

Sara had thought she might follow the same course. But she had never once imagined a situation like this one. Was she taking it too seriously? Those village women seemed to think she should be pleased to have a free afternoon . . .

It seemed a very long afternoon. At last Sara decided to go out again. Why not look in on Mrs Hendry? Yes, as a fellow teacher, Mrs Hendry might agree with her conviction that this Tattie Planting Holiday was just a bit of nonsense which should be scrapped. Feeling more cheerful, she set off.

"Oh, no, dear, that would never do!" protested Mrs Hendry, after hearing Sara's views. "It's gone on as long as anyone remembers, and what harm does it do if the bairns have one extra afternoon to play after all?"

A MOTHER'S PLEA

A MOTHER whispering to herself at bedtime the opening of the 139th Psalm. How close is God.

'Twas the night her only son had left home for London. So young. Would city lights be a fatal lure? Many were her counsels and her parting gift a Bible.

"If ever in trouble, turn up the 139th Psalm!" A curious plea, he felt.

But things went well; his being, like a flower, opened to city life. Entrancing new freedoms he did not abuse.

No trouble came his way. His Bible lay unopened. So he never turned up the 139th Psalm. Never found the £5 note his mother had slipped in at the very page.

Till long, long afterwards!

Rev. T. R. S. Campbell.

"Why didn't you warn me about it?" Sara asked crisply. "I didn't know what the children were going on about when they spoke of it."

Mrs Hendry blinked at her tone.

"I never thought but that you would know," she admitted. "Everyone in Tillydrem knows . . ."

"Well, please tell me about any other extraordinary thing likely to happen," returned Sara. "I really must have advance warning next time."

LEAVING Mrs Hendry, she decided to go for a good, long walk. It was light for longer now and the day was certainly ending with a fine, mild evening.

She sauntered on towards the river path, passing a small group of children with bunches of primroses. Eagerly they displayed their flowers to their teacher, plainly having forgotten that she didn't want them to have a holiday at all.

Oh, well, she had better take the Gillons' advice and overlook the whole thing, Sara decided. It was more important to remain on friendly terms with the youngsters. She began to plan the things she would do with them next week, and gradually some of the peace of the evening came into her heart.

This river path was really charming, with the late sunshine flickering through the trees. And how wonderful it was to feel one could walk along in safety, even if quite alone. Lonely river walks near big towns weren't considered too safe these days.

Voices broke into her musings. She looked ahead and saw what was obviously the fishing party returning to the village. Yes, there was Brian Gillon, Peter Munro and Bill Matheson. Little Sandy Gillon was there, too, alongside a stalwart young man who must be the uncle from Glasgow.

At first glimpse, Sara realised he wasn't the type she'd imagined. There was nothing scruffy about his casual clothes, and as he got nearer she realised he was older than she had expected, perhaps in his late twenties.

Like the others, these pupils bore no grudge against her, but ran forward eagerly, describing how two fish had been caught, one by little Sandy.

"I'll show you," offered Sandy, opening what Sara saw with disapproval was his school bag, and revealing one small, wet trout.

"I got a bigger one," Brian boasted. "And I know how to do it now, so I'll be able to go and catch lots by myself."

"I nearly got a huge one," exclaimed Bill Matheson.

"So did I . . . nearly," Peter cried.

How excited they all were, and how friendly, Sara thought, then she found herself looking into the amused grey eyes of the young man.

"Are you Miss Milton?" he asked. "As my nephew has no thought of introducing us, I'll just say I'm their uncle, Charles Gillon . . ."

"Yes, I realise that," Sara cut in.

Remembering what she had wanted to say to this young man, she drew a deep breath, then went on.

"Brian gave me your message," she informed him coldly. "I may say I don't in the least approve of this ridiculous holiday, and will do my best to stop it in future. Surely you could have had the fishing expedition on Saturday. But no, Brian says you're going to a protest march and hoping it'll turn into a riot."

She stopped, realising Brian hadn't said anything about "hoping." The grey eyes were looking back at her now with surprise.

"I know my nephew Brian doesn't always explain things properly," Charles Gillon said after a moment. "Did he really say I was hoping for a riot?"

Sara knew she was blushing.

"Well, you said there might be a riot, something like that," she got out. "I may as well tell you I'm against those protest marches. I don't think they are a good idea at all."

"Like the Tattie Planting Holiday isn't a good idea?" he returned.

"Come on, Uncle Charles," Brian was shouting back. "You said you would show me how to clean my fish, then we can have it for supper."

"I'd better go," Charles said. "But one word of advice, Miss Milton. Things aren't always what they seem!"

He smiled, then strode off, leaving Sara gazing after him in perplexity. What on earth did he mean? She felt uneasy. What wasn't what it seemed?

OH, forget it, she told herself, and now out of tune with the fine evening, she turned and made for the schoolhouse. But once there she found concentration on anything difficult. She corrected essays, turned on the television, then switched it off impatiently, finally deciding to settle with an interesting historical novel she'd got from the travelling library last week.

After three pages Sara became aware that she hadn't taken in what she had read. Really, whatever was the matter with her? She kept thinking of those grey eyes looking right into hers, and the way the young man had spoken.

How absurd! She'd do better to put him right out of her mind if he was the protest-march type. No, she would never want to know that kind, however good the cause for the protest might be. Were there not other ways of bringing things to public notice?

By the next evening, she felt calmer about everything. Why, she might never see Charles Gillon again! Or did he come often to Tillydrem? To stop herself wondering, she put on the television, getting a brief view of the protest march that afternoon. At one point there had been a scuffle and several people had been injured.

So he did get a riot, Sara thought. She began to wonder if he was one of the people who had been hurt. No, he seemed the sort who could look after himself. He'd be all right, she felt sure!

It was Mrs Munro who gave her the news next morning, joining her as she walked to church.

"I'm wondering how the minister will manage the service today," said the stout woman. "Did you hear his young brother got hurt in that march they had in Glasgow yesterday? Ay, they took him to hospital, too."

She shook her head gloomily, then paused to wait for her friend Mrs Boyd. Sara walked on. She still didn't approve of the march, but she felt strangely concerned because that grey-eyed young man with the pleasant smile had been hurt.

After the service she found herself loitering about, to waylay the minister as he left the church. Mr Gillon had taken the service quite normally, not at all as if he was worried by what had happened to his brother. But then, perhaps he was just putting on a brave face.

Everyone else had gone home when at last he emerged.

"Well, Sara," he greeted her. "Another fine day, just like it was for the holiday afternoon."

His eyes twinkled, so surely that meant Charles Gillon wasn't much injured. But she still wanted to know.

"I met your brother that evening," she told the minister. "I hear he came to grief in the march yesterday. Why on earth does he go to such things?" she burst out. "He even said he thought there would be trouble."

Mr Gillon looked back at her in obvious surprise.

"Charles had to go yesterday," he replied. "Perhaps you haven't heard what he does. He's a policeman and, though he should have been free, his leave was cancelled because of the march. That's why he came here on Friday."

SARA wished the ground would open and swallow her quickly. What a fool she had been! She'd assumed that Charles Gillon must be a heedless, irresponsible type, all because his young nephew said he was going to a riot. Even when she saw him she'd never guessed he might be a policeman, working hard to keep law and order.

"Is . . . is he badly hurt?" she faltered.

"Oh, no," replied the minister. "Just a rather unsightly bruise on his face where he was hit by a stone. In fact, he's been given a few days' leave, so came up here late last night. This morning he's having a well-earned long lie. Would you like to come along later and meet him properly, Sara? Do join us for tea."

Sara almost refused, then suddenly felt she must go. Ought she not to explain to Charles Gillon why she had spoken to him so critically? Yes, she must.

Tea at the Manse prove to be a lively affair, with the boys chattering away while she kept quiet. Then afterwards all at once she found herself alone with the young man. Now was her chance.

"I owe you an apology," she managed to say. "I didn't realise you were in the Police Force."

"Was that it?" he broke in. "I wondered why you were so down on me for going to be at the march. It's the last thing I wanted to do!"

"I'm sorry," Sara whispered. "Please forgive me."

"On one condition!"

"What is it?" she asked uncertainly.

"That you stop being cross about the Tattie Planting Holiday, and learn to love all the funny customs and traditions that make Tillydrem so unique and wonderful. Will you do that, Sara?"

"Yes," she said. "Yes, I promise I will."

A smile was exchanged — a warm, friendly smile that made her no longer the severe schoolteacher who liked everything done her way. She became, in fact, a girl who was just putting a first step on a road she had never gone before — the road to romance. □

Miracle For Four

by FRANCES SOMERVILLE

I DO not know why I felt so deprived after coming to live at Whiteacres. I'd always loved the house as a child.

It had belonged to my maiden Aunt Bridget, then. The outside world might have considered her rather eccentric, but to my sister, Mhairi, and me she was a deliverer.

We lived with our parents in a grime-coated town. Father worked at the mine as overseer, and our house was grey and grim within sight of the workings. It was a town to get away from and our trips into the country to stay with Aunt Bridget were the highlights of our life.

Whiteacres had a garden which, to us, resembled a public park. It was filled with shrubs and tall trees and every flower imaginable.

Aunt Bridget had a way with plants. She talked to them incessantly, pleading with them to flourish — and they did.

Her herb garden was filled with sweet fragrances but our favourite spot was the secret garden behind the toolshed. Here, Mhairi and I would play for hours among old-fashioned roses, tall hollyhocks and every flower we told Aunt Bridget we liked.

The secret garden was rarely weeded, because if a weed showed any sort of flower we claimed this as our own, too. There were curling bracken and coltsfoot and dandelions and daisies and even nettles.

When we heard about Aunt Bridget's legacy, we were living in London. My business was centred there; I was becoming respected as a designer of original knitwear.

There was a second reason. Mhairi's eyesight had been deteriorating rapidly over the last five years, and now it had reached a critical stage.

I had taken her to every eye specialist in the city, and they all agreed. There was only one operation which could restore her sight — but if it didn't work it would destroy what little she had left.

Mhairi remained undecided. It was not that she lacked courage, but she admitted to me that she would rather have one tiny window into the world than be condemned to total darkness.

I suggested to Mhairi that we sell Whiteacres. The money, I explained, would buy a house within commuting distance of London, and fit it with all those gadgets that would make Mhairi's life easier. I really believed I was being considerate until I heard her intake of breath.

"You haven't forgotten Aunt Bridget's herb garden, have you, Joanie?" she asked accusingly. "Or our trees? Our secret garden?"

No, of course I hadn't forgotten. But were they not just fantasies from our childhood?

Aunt Bridget's herbs. How could I forget those? I crossed to the bookshelf and pulled out my old Bible. Inside I found pale sprigs of thyme, a leaf of sage and a flattened clump of rosemary.

"You *haven't* forgotten," my sister remarked evenly. I'd forgotten how acute Mhairi's sense of smell had become since her eyesight failed.

A NYWAY, I decided to take Mhairi for a ride in the car that afternoon and we drove all the way down to Whiteacres. I pushed open the rusty gate and turned to help Mhairi but she was already forging ahead. She seemed to remember every step of the way, as though the garden remained imprinted in her mind.

Perhaps it was as well she could not see the extent of the devastation in Aunt Bridget's garden. Over the years the place had been overrun with weeds and the roses had mostly gone to briar now.

"Oh, Joanie," Mhairi was saying wistfully, "can't you smell the apple blossom? I bet I'm walking on a carpet of pink petals. Remember how we used to fill little bags with them and hang them in our wardrobe?"

Mhairi was a child again, vivacious and eager. It did my heart good to see her like this.

A tall bay hedge and a taller stone wall separated Whiteacres from a neighbouring villa and somewhere over there, I could hear grass being mowed. Once again, it seemed, Mhairi's memory was stirred. She began to giggle.

"Remember old Colonel Sourpuss, Joanie?"

When we were small my aunt's neighbour had been a retired colonel from the Indian Army. Colonel Sourple, she explained anxiously, disliked invasions on his privacy. We christened him Sourpuss after our first confrontation.

Aunt Bridget was a kind woman. She knew how children could become bored, even in such splendid surroundings, and she had arranged for part of the garden to be cleared and a net strung across the centre. There we could play our own particular brand of tennis.

It was my backhand that did it. Up went the ball skywards, over the bay hedge and then the 10-foot wall. Then we heard a sound of tinkling glass.

Mhairi and I stood trembling with apprehension, and Aunt Bridget came running out from the house. Even she seemed slightly nervous.

"You had better go round and apologise. Tell the colonel that I will pay for the repair of any damage."

Easily enough said, of course, but ever since coming to Whiteacres, Mhairi and I had, in our spare moments, been making up all sorts of grim stories about Auntie's neighbour and the woodshed.

"Well, go on, dears," Aunt Bridget urged.

So off we slunk, keeping close to the hedge all along the lane until we reached the tall gates. The handle would not turn and we were about to turn tail when a voice rang out.

"Did you want something, please?"

The boy was about my own age and had the thickest, blackest hair I had ever seen.

"We've come about the colonel's glasshouse," I explained in a trembling voice.

The boy looked at me loftily. "So that was you?

"By the way," the boy said, "I'm Garry Sourple. I'll go and tell Father you've called."

We were shown into the conservatory soon after that and my garrulous sister had to go and explain all about our game of tennis. The boy began to grin at me.

"Must have been some backhand that — to sail over our wall. Eh, Father?"

Colonel Sourpuss scowled at us from below his thick black brows.

He made us sit down on high-backed chairs and interrogated us like raw recruits. Then he rasped out an order to his son, who hurried away to fetch us fizzy drinks.

He possibly was not such a bad old boy, the colonel, it was just his regimental manner that frightened us. We gave the woodshed a wide berth on our way out.

After that, we'd occasionally catch a glimpse of the Sourples when Aunt Bridget took us to church.

The colonel and his son had their own special pew at the back of the church. Garry always looked rather lonely, I felt, sitting poker-backed beside his austere parent.

The mine where our father worked closed down and we emigrated to Canada. We spent 10 years abroad before returning to the UK, when, to our sorrow, we learned Aunt Bridget had had a stroke and gone to live in a nursing home.

Mhairi and I often visited her during the last year of her life. Although she could hardly speak, we would talk about the old days and she would smile happily. We did not know until her death that she had willed her house to us both.

SO now we were back at Whiteacres. Mhairi was in her element, and I could not bear to tell her how the house had deteriorated.

Perhaps we could do something with it — but it would take a lot of money. Would it be possible, I wondered, to carry on my business from the country? After all, knitting designs could be thought up anywhere and I could have all my equipment sent down and make one of the guest rooms into a workshop . . .

This was what I had been doing for the past three months. There were drawbacks, of course, but all in all, we were managing.

Once a month I would drive to London to collect orders, visit the design centres, and have a look at the latest trends in wool and fashion. Then I'd drive home laden with parcels. Each time I arrived back, Mhairi would be waiting to greet me. It made everything worth while just to catch sight of her beaming face.

"Guess who I was speaking to yesterday," she boasted after my last trip. "Garry Sourple!"

"Good gracious. The colonel's son? Do they still live next door?"

Mhairi's face saddened.

"The colonel died four years ago, and Garry just uses the house whenever he gets leave from hospital. He's a surgeon now."

Mhairi's face turned slightly pink as she told me how Garry had come round to borrow some petrol for his lawnmower. He'd promised to replace it next weekend.

I could see an expression on my sister's face that told me she had more to tell me but she said nothing until we were sitting eating our evening meal.

"Garry knows a lot about that eye operation. He says it's carried out regularly in his hospital, and there's a much higher percentage of success these days."

"Really?"

I could not help it if I sounded sceptical. I had been trying, without success, to coax Mhairi into having that operation.

"I told Garry I'd think about it, Joanie."

I was being unfair. What did it matter whose idea it was, so long as Mhairi made the right decision?

NEXT morning was Saturday and I could hear the mower at work on the other side of the wall.

I tried to picture Garry. How would he look today? I remembered him as being rather small — but then I had been big for my age and stood a head taller than him.

When I asked Mhairi for her impressions all she could say was that he had a lovely rich baritone voice and smelt of after-shave. So, after she went for her afternoon nap, I sneaked out of the house and got the old wooden ladder out of the shed.

The skirt I was wearing was of my own design — straight, with a slit up one side and made from fine grey wool. Certainly not the outfit for such exploits, but I was determined.

Eventually I was on the top rung with both hands on the stone coping. I gazed down into a wilderness almost as impossible as ours at Whiteacres.

I watched a long rangy figure walking to and fro between the apple trees, dallying where the rye grass persisted. He looked gorgeous, just the sort of man I have a weakness for, with that shock of black hair and such a lean, interesting face. I leaned forward and watched intently.

As he turned the machine and came towards me I decided to duck out of sight, but as I moved backwards one of the fancy coping stones began to rock backwards and forwards. I perched on the ladder petrified with fear, and watched it topple forward.

I shut my eyes as it plummeted downwards. Then there was this almighty crash and when I opened my eyes I watched the colonel's greenhouse disintegrate pane by pane.

"Do you make a habit of doing that?" Garry Sourple asked without a trace of malice in his voice.

He grinned up at my alarmed expression. "That old thing was due to come down anyway. You've just saved me the cost of demolition."

Garry invited me to join him and placed a ladder against his side of the wall. He watched with much interest as I tried to descend gracefully in my tight-fitting grey skirt.

THEN we were talking sixteen to the dozen; talking as we had never talked in our youth. I explained all about my business and how I had a regular clientele in the city. Garry seemed most impressed.

He told me how he had studied medicine and how his father had been so proud to see him graduate.

Finally he explained how he had been appointed surgeon in one of our city's largest hospitals. That, of course, brought us back to Mhairi again.

"She really should have that op., Joanie. I know a very good man. I could easily have a word."

Before the visit was over I'd invited Garry across for dinner that evening. I went home already planning something really special to impress him. I kept trying to convince myself I was doing it all for Mhairi, but each time I looked into Garry's eyes I knew that I was fooling nobody.

That night, as we sat at the table, my sister never stopped talking. I hadn't heard her sound so animated in years.

It also meant that I was free to study Garry. I found him very attractive; not handsome in the regular meaning of the word, but distinctive and with a bearing that I was sure would impress patients to trust in him. I could see Mhairi was smitten, too.

From the day I started looking after my sister my social life began to deteriorate. There had only ever been one man in my life who had asked me to marry him.

Miles Lorenson attended the same textile college as me, but he had been offered a marvellous opportunity to work in Paris. Miles wanted me to go with him — as his wife — and then go into business together. Unfortunately his plans did not include Mhairi, and I put the offer out of my mind.

Now, once more, I found myself in love. This time it was with Garry Sourple and once more it seemed my position was doomed to failure.

It was obvious to me that Mhairi also had fallen for Garry. She could talk from morning until night about him and never run out of praises.

"Garry said this to me." "Garry said that." "Oh, Joanie, isn't he wonderful?"

If I grew rather silent on the topic of Garry, Mhairi did not seem to notice. For the first time since she lost her sight, she had discovered something worthwhile to hang on to. How could I possibly undermine that?

A FEW DAYS AGO, Mhairi underwent her operation and the bandages are due to be removed today.

I was filled with apprehension as I drove to the city. If Mhairi's operation was a success, our two lives would be altered drastically. But what if it wasn't a success? What would happen then?

The sister in charge smiled at me encouragingly as she led me along the white-walled corridor.

"Mhairi's big day at last." She spoke confidently but did nothing to reassure me.

When I entered the small ward Mhairi was already sitting up in bed and looking at me . . . yes, really looking. The unbandaging had taken place in the early hours.

We cried a lot, Mhairi and I, and hugged each other for a long, long time, then she began to talk about the surgeon who had performed her miracle for her. His name was Josh Bluett and he was the most wonderful person she had ever met.

She spoke of her magician in the way she had once enthused over Garry. When I could get a word in I mentioned his name.

"Garry?" my sister echoed, "Of course, he's been round — several times, in fact. He said he had to see me through until the end.

"He's ever such a nice man, Garry, don't you think? I think he fancies you. He was always talking about you when he came across to Whiteacres."

Mhairi went on and on, but I had no wish to interrupt. It gave me time to analyse my own thoughts, time to make up my mind what I would say when Garry came across at the weekend to join our celebration dinner.

Suddenly it seemed the sun had risen in my life once more. It was not just Mhairi for whom the world had become a lovely place. □

MUCKLE ROE

Off the west of Mainland Shetland, Muckle Roe is ringed by high, red granite cliffs. Apart from a small crofting community, the island is a patchwork of moorland and water, offering a bonus to walkers. Another bonus for summer visitors to Shetland is the "simmer dim," the long days when there is never true darkness. In addition to the vistas over tiny, green, uninhabited islands from Muckle Roe to Eshaness and its lighthouse, and Sandness where the Papa Stour boat sails from three times a week, a day of good visibility can give a sighting of Foula, 14 miles out to the West, Britain's remotest inhabited island.

MUCKLE ROE, SHETLAND

ONE afternoon in May, Judy Fraser walked up the garden path of Glenhead Cottage and crossed the busy road to the safety and delights of the fields beyond.

Around her was the scene she had known all her life. The hawthorn flourish, as Granny Fraser called the blossom, had never been more prolific. Over there, with the sun filtering through the trees, the wild hyacinths formed a carpet of the most exquisite beauty.

Then, suddenly, this fair-haired girl of 20 stumbled, as tears blinded her. For this would be the last time she would gaze on her surroundings as they were now. When spring came round next year, all this loveliness would have vanished, devoured by the new road that was pitilessly drawing nearer every day.

But the most heart-rending blow of all was the knowledge that Glenhead Cottage, her beloved home, was also right in the path of this approaching monster and, in due course, would be bulldozed into rubble.

Judy opened the gate to the wood and wandered over to a fallen tree.

She sat down. This had always been one of her favourite spots, a place of magic. Here, as a child, she had brought her secrets and shared them with all sorts of imaginary people. Now, she was bringing her sadness and her fears for the future.

Through a gap in the trees, she gazed at Glenhead Cottage. Judy had been three weeks old when her parents had died in a car crash. Granny had brought the baby here to her home on the outskirts of the village of Glengask, lavishing all her love on this, her only remaining relative.

The formative years for Judy passed with an ever-growing affection between the elderly woman and the child. They were everything to each other.

Judy attended the village school, followed by a few years of higher education in Perth. She was a naturally clever girl and Granny was proud to subsidise a further course in

60

THE PRICE OF LOVE

by Nan Baxter

business studies. Nothing was too good for this lovely, precious bairn.

But money was tight, so up went a bed and breakfast board. The result for Judy was a new confidence and a good job in an insurance office in the town, travelling out and in daily by bus.

And it gave Granny the satisfaction of seeing Judy develop into a young woman of natural charm and considerable beauty. If Granny Fraser was inclined to be a little possessive at times, who would blame her?

And now, what? Judy recalled the first time they had learned their home was threatened. That was two years ago, with a map appearing in the local paper and a thick black line crossing all that they loved. Consternation had turned to anger and then, as time went on, resignation.

Official notice had come, eventually, and there was the offer of rehousing or compensation. It had never entered Judy's mind that Granny would want to leave the district.

"I wouldn't like to stay in another house about here," she told Judy, one winter evening when the snow had drifted and stopped the traffic on the glen road. "It could never take the place of this one, with all its memories. Mind you, I'll hate leaving Glengask and all my friends."

Somehow, the quietness encouraged confidences.

"You know that I was brought up on a farm near Aberdeen," the old lady went on, "but I don't think I ever told you that I met your grandfather in Edinburgh. I was a cook in a big house and John was a joiner. He fancied working in the country and managed to find a job in Glengask here. We were lucky to get Glenhead Cottage."

Granny's faded blue eyes had misted.

"He died just six months before your father and mother were killed in that accident. I thought I'd never stay on here, but when you came I'd something to live for. But now that you're grown up —"

She was eyeing Judy closely.

"I've thought a lot about this, and it may seem strange to you, but I've got a hankering to go back to Edinburgh. And I think it would be a good thing for you.

"With your qualifications, I'm sure you'd get a better job, you'd meet interesting people. And some day, Judy, you'll marry, although I'll be loth to let you go."

"Then the man I marry," declared Judy, "must love you, too."

They had laughed at that, and no more was said about the future. Like Granny, Judy knew she would be sick at heart when she left the glen, but she must be realistic, and the thought of moving to Edinburgh appealed to her. Meantime, it was as if nature had made a special effort this spring for her benefit. And she must savour it to the full.

JUDY stood up and took a deep breath of the sweet, scented air. Spring was so exciting. She held her head high, threw out her arms as if she were welcoming someone, revelling in the ecstasy of it all. Then, a few steps of a dance, and she started to sing, as loudly as she could, "The hills are alive with the sound of music."

For a minute or two, she lost herself in this simple childlike rapture. Then she saw the young man and, embarrassed, stopped abruptly.

He was standing there, only a short distance away, a tall, slightly indistinct figure in the shadows of the trees.

Judy held her breath. He wasn't a local man, she knew. Who was he? This wood had always been her own preserve.

They regarded each other for what seemed ages until, suddenly, he was coming towards her.

With a little cry, Judy started to run. But he was quick to follow her. "It's all right," he called out. "Don't be afraid."

He had a nice voice, and as he reached her side, she saw he was smiling.

"You're Judy Fraser, aren't you?" he asked, and some of her panic left her.

"Yes," she answered, in surprise. "Who are you?"

"I'm Dick Rutherford," he replied. He had a well-shaped face and fine, steady eyes. "I saw you at the village dance last week, and asked someone your name."

Yes, and he must have asked, too, where she stayed, considered Judy, and felt flattered.

He was smiling to her, a little timidly, but obviously anxious to continue the conversation.

"You've got a lovely singing voice," he said. "I'm sorry I gave you such a fright. I was standing, listening and watching you, for quite a time. You looked so happy."

"I always enjoy the wood." Judy gave a little laugh. "You must have thought me crazy."

A THOUGHT struck Judy. There were quite a few young men in the village these days who were strangers.

"Where is your home?" she asked. "You must be new to the district."

"My home is in Glasgow," he told her, "but while I'm working around here my company put me up in the hotel. I'm a surveyor on the new road."

"Yes, I rather guessed you were." Judy was regarding him coldly. "Not exactly the most popular type of man with some of the local people, especially the farmers."

"I agree, but then, I'm only an employee." Dick Rutherford's dark eyes were pleading with her. "After all, sooner or later, this road had to come."

"And this lovely wood to disappear," she reminded him, "and, more important, people's homes. Come over here and I'll show you the only home I've ever known."

They looked across to Glenhead Cottage.

"I love that place, and so does my grandmother. You can imagine how we feel about it being knocked down."

He looked genuinely concerned.

Judy knew it was unfair to lay the blame for this catastrophe at his feet, but her feelings were running high and quite difficult to control.

Yet she couldn't but admire this man's resilience as he continued.

"That glen road can't carry today's traffic," he insisted. "It's dangerous, with all these bends. And I don't need to tell you of the high accident rate."

That was true enough. Many an injured person had been brought in to Glenhead Cottage, to wait until an ambulance arrived.

They didn't talk much after that, but, undaunted, Dick made one last effort to strike up a friendship.

"The next dance in the hall is on Friday," he said. "Are you going?"

"I haven't thought of it," parried Judy.

So they left it at that.

Heading back to Glenhead Cottage, Judy's thoughts were completely centred round Dick Rutherford. He was possibly the most handsome man she had ever met, with an undoubted charm.

Yes, she decided, it would be fun to meet him again and dispel some of that coolness she had shown him. Meantime, her encounter in the bluebell wood would be the first secret she had ever kept from Granny.

So You Think You Know About Wales?

1. In which castle was Prince Charles invested as Prince of Wales?
2. Which castle is surrounded by water on three sides?
3. Which castle shares its name with a famous cheese?

Answers below.

1. *Caernarvon.*
2. *Pembroke.*
3. *Caerphilly.*

THERE was a touch of mischievousness in Judy's eyes when she met Dick Rutherford again on Friday evening. He responded with such a look of surprised delight that he immediately took her in his arms and they began to dance.

The hall was packed, and on this warm spring evening, it was refreshing to escape from the noise and go outside to the fresh air. Slowly, they walked up the back road to the old bridge that spanned the burn, and sat down.

Conversation flowed freely. Dick's parents were both teachers, he told Judy, and he was an only child. He was keen on his job and loved the open air.

With Judy, there was even less to tell, for there was only Granny in her life. She emphasised Granny's bitterness about the new road, and told of their decision to move to Edinburgh.

"You must meet my grandmother," she said, having already decided to tell Granny of Dick's existence. "I warn you, she's almost certain to be difficult. But let me also tell you she has a heart of gold and, for me, is the most wonderful woman in the world."

The result was that, a week later, Dick was invited to supper.

That evening, Granny Fraser was pointedly polite to the young man. She provided an excellent meal and there was no mention of the road until, the supper over, they sat round the fire.

The old lady braced her shoulders as she regarded Dick. Then she went straight to the point.

"I'm glad to have a word with you," she said. "You're not to blame, but you're still an agent for all this destruction.

"I hear that the gift shop is selling out, frightened by the loss of trade when the village is to be by-passed. Perhaps it's just a coincidence, but the minister, old Mr Kirkland, is retiring too, after thirty years in the parish. He was a great comfort to me when John died."

There was no stopping this resolute woman.

"But now, this business of the road is getting on my nerves," she declared vehemently, "and I just can't settle. The sooner we're away from here the better.

"I've had my say, and you know how I feel. Now let's talk of other things. Do you play golf?" she asked Dick.

Judy gave a sigh of relief. Her fears of Granny's reception of Dick had proved groundless. But neither had she displayed any real pleasure.

SUMMER progressed, and Granny was busy with her bed and breakfasts. Judy lent a helping hand, but there was still plenty of time for Dick and her to walk to Scott's View and back, have an evening at the theatre in Perth, or perhaps a run round Loch Leven in Dick's car.

Sometimes, on those long clear nights, it was fun to get into the car and set off, not knowing where they would end up.

That was what they were going to do one evening when Dick had arrived early at Glenhead Cottage to wait for Judy coming home from her job. A quick tidy-up, and she would be ready to go.

"Judy should be here by now," Granny was saying. "Some friends are giving her a lift in their car."

They were sitting on a garden seat, watching the traffic go by.

"Look at that madman," Granny called out, "racing along as if the devil himself were after him! No wonder there are accidents."

She turned to Dick.

"I've seen you speeding, too," she lectured. "Now, promise you'll be careful tonight."

"I promise," Dick assured her, and with that they heard the screech of brakes, a loud, frightening noise, and then a deadly silence.

"It's an accident — down there by the corner!" Granny gripped Dick's arm. "I've heard that sound so often."

They started to run up the garden path.

"Pray God it's not Judy." Granny's face was pale, and she was trembling. "You go on and I'll follow."

A couple, looking stunned, were sitting on the verge. One car was still on the road, but badly crushed, another was on its side. It was there Dick saw Judy, her body free, but her legs obviously trapped.

He was on his knees immediately.

She was in pain, but managed a smile. "Just get the weight off me."

By now, there was quite a queue of cars, and people were gathering to help. Quickly, Dick, with some other men, managed to lift the car sufficiently so that Judy could be drawn free. Someone had already set off to the village to contact the police and the doctor.

IT seemed ages before the police arrived, followed by the doctor, and then the ambulance. Judy and the other two must go to hospital, the doctor decided.

Granny stood, watching the ambulance. She was numb with fear.

But Dick was by her side. He took her arm. "I suggest you collect some of the things that Judy will need, and we'll both go to the hospital."

"That's good of you." Granny leaned heavily on him. Without Dick Rutherford's guidance, she would have been completely lost.

At the hospital, they did not see Judy. She was still under examination.

"Ring in the morning," a nurse suggested, and they left, disappointed.

Granny was unusually quiet on the return journey. Only when they were approaching Glenhead Cottage did she begin to talk freely.

"Come away in," she said. "You've had nothing to eat for ages. You must be starving. Will cold ham and a salad suit you?"

"Super," answered Dick, and he was quick to recognise Granny's new and kindly approach towards him.

All through the meal, their thoughts centred on Judy.

"I wonder how she's getting on," pondered Granny. "This is the first time we've been separated, even for a night. No doubt Judy told you how she came to me."

"Yes," Dick answered, "and she told me, too, of her love for you, and her deep gratitude for all you have done for her."

"She's all I've got." Granny played with her food.

"Tell me," she added suddenly, and looked searchingly at Dick, "you care a lot for Judy?"

"I love her with all my heart," he answered simply.

They talked on for a time, until Dick rose to his feet.

"You're tired," he said. "Have a good night's sleep and I'll collect you tomorrow in time for the evening visiting hours."

WHEN Dick and Granny saw Judy, it was to find a pale, but remarkably bright young woman.

"I've been lucky," she told them.

They talked until their bedside conversation dried up, and they were searching for something to say. But Judy was not finished.

"I had a visit this morning from Mr Kirkland. Sunday is his last day in Glengask Church. I wish I could be there." She looked up at Dick.

The Price Of Love

"Will you go and take Granny with you? I know she'd like that."

And so it came about that on Sunday morning, Dick and Granny Fraser climbed the outside stair to the gallery of the church.

It was a simple service, with the singing of old, familiar psalms and hymns, and readings from well-known chapters of the Bible. Prayers, then the sermon when everyone seemed to sit up in expectation.

Mr Kirkland started off bravely. "Farewell, I wish you all joy. This is my message to you today, and it is not one of sadness.

"Christian faith is all about happiness."

Yes, considered Granny, she should certainly take this to heart. For hadn't she been selfish, making herself unhappy in going out of her way to deny happiness to Judy and Dick? And now she knew with certainty that the young couple were deeply in love with each other.

"Count your blessings."

Yes, she would do that all right. She was lucky. She had Judy and now, in her new way of thinking, she had Dick, too.

A prayer of thanksgiving, and the service was over. Soon a queue was forming to shake hands with Mr Kirkland at the door.

"Mrs Fraser!" He held her hand tightly. "Thank you for your friendship over all those years. Judy is getting on well, I know. And you're the boyfriend?"

He was looking at Dick, but it was Granny who replied.

"Yes, Dick Rutherford is going to play a big part in our lives now. And today you've helped me to appreciate him. Bless you."

As Granny walked towards the car, lots of people came up to speak to her, and she had a word or two for them all.

At last, they got into the car, and were soon back at Glenhead Cottage.

"It's been quite a morning," Granny said, as she got out. And an emotional one, too, she considered. "There's a lot to tell Judy, and I think you should go on your own to the hospital today. I'm sure you've things to tell her that need privacy."

"Thank you." Dick was smiling. "I've just been thinking, isn't it rather odd that without the building of the new road, Judy and I would never have met?"

"God moves in a mysterious way," Granny declared, and promptly kissed the young man. □

The Homecoming

by ELSPETH RAE

FIONA BOYD was sitting on the bed biting her nails (a bad habit to which she only succumbed in times of stress) when her sister, Eileen, popped her head round the door and called excitedly, "Andy's here, Fi. Are you ready?"

"Yes," she said in a whisper, which was all that she could summon up. "Do I look all right?"

"Marvellous!" Eileen assured her. "That shirt's a lovely shade of blue."

"It's ridiculous," Fiona said as they started downstairs together. "I'm so nervous! Why, I don't know — I should be radiantly happy, seeing my boyfriend again after a year! But I'm shaking inside!"

"You've been under a strain, ever since Michael's accident," Eileen said sympathetically, taking her sister's arm. "I don't know how you bore up as well as you did!"

"It was Andy who helped me to do that!" Fiona replied. "He saw to it that I heard every single piece of news as soon as it came through from America. Mr and Mrs Hall were often too upset to remember, poor souls! But Andy always did."

A moment later she smiled at Andy Hall as she slid into the front seat of the car beside him.

"Well?" she asked anxiously. "How is he? How did he stand the flight?"

"Fine," Andy assured her with a grin. "He's sitting beside the fire enjoying the fuss Mum and Dad are making of him. He can move along quite smartly, too. He was practising with his sticks before he left hospital."

As the car stopped at traffic lights, Fiona glanced at her companion.

"He won't always have to walk with sticks, will he?" she asked waveringly, remembering Michael's confident, long-strided walk, and his love of sport. She just could not imagine him resigning himself to disability.

"Oh no!" Andy said firmly. "It'll take time, though. Both legs were badly broken, remember."

Remember? How would she ever forget that autumn evening when Andy had arrived at the door, ashen faced, to tell her about Michael's accident? She could not take in the extent of his injuries at first. Only a

week before she had seen him off on the train to London, on the first stage of his journey to Canada. She had not even had time to receive a letter from him.

"Come on, Daydreamer!" Andy's amused voice broke into her reflections. They had arrived at the Halls' bungalow.

"My legs have gone all wobbly!" Fiona exclaimed shakily as she got out of the car.

"Here!" Andy tucked her arm into his in a brotherly gesture. "Hang on. You can faint as soon as you've said, 'Welcome home.' "

However, Fiona didn't faint when she set eyes on Michael. She burst into tears instead.

"And I thought she'd be glad to see me!" Michael quipped with an embarrassed little laugh, as he held his hands out to her.

He'd lost weight, Fiona noted, but it hadn't detracted from his good looks. If anything, it accentuated them. As she squeezed his hands, his blue eyes smiled into hers.

"Sorry," she apologised. "It's been a long wait."

"And a very worrying one." Mrs Hall came over to lay a comforting hand on Fiona's shoulder. "I did just the same when I first saw him."

"How about a glass of sherry?" Andy suggested. "As a celebration?"

"Good idea," Mr Hall said eagerly.

Fiona caught the sardonic glint in Michael's eye that she remembered so well; it told her what he thought of his family's idea of a celebration.

It had been just this sort of thing that had driven him to take the Canadian job in the first place. Really, when she thought about it, she supposed Michael looked down on his family for their homely little ways.

An hour later, she was ready to leave. As she bent to kiss her boyfriend she noticed his expression was markedly strained.

It's understandable if he's short tempered, she told herself. He's still not fit and probably still in pain.

"I'll come again tomorrow," she told him cheerfully. "You'll be more rested by then. I can tell you everything that's been happening while you've been away."

"You mean that will take longer than five minutes?" Michael asked.

"Slightly," Fiona replied evenly.

A S Andy drove away from the gate, he said quietly, "I'll see you two are left on your own tomorrow evening. I'll have a word in Mum's ear."

"Thanks." Fiona smiled.

Silence fell. Andy broke it eventually.

"He always was the impatient one of the family," he began awkwardly. "I expect he'll be a bit difficult now he's convalescing."

Turning to her companion, Fiona noticed that his cheeks were quite pink. It suddenly dawned on her that Andy had been hurt by his brother's attitude, and she felt a pang of sympathy for him.

"And you were always the patient one," she said gently. "All those hours you spent up at the Kingfisher Pool! Did you ever see it again?"

Andy shook his head and they fell silent again. This time it was a companionable silence as they shared precious childhood memories.

The story of the Kingfisher Pool had started one bright June day. Andy, Fiona and Michael (two 10-year-olds and a bossy 12-year-old) had been wandering along the Waterworks Road looking for wild flowers for a school project.

It had been Andy's and Fiona's project, strictly speaking. Michael had only come along for want of better things to do.

As they approached the Old Brig, Miss Thomson, the minister's housekeeper, had come struggling up the bank and beckoned wildly to them.

They soon found out the cause of her excitement. A bird, the most beautiful bird Fiona had ever seen, with blue-green and orange plumage, was sitting on a branch overlooking the pool.

"What is it?" Andy had whispered, enraptured.

"Shh . . . it's a kingfisher," Miss Thomson told them, softly. "You hardly ever see one in those parts."

They watched the bird for what had seemed hours, then Michael lost patience and deliberately clapped his hands to scare it.

Miss Thomson had been furious, and Andy had looked as though he were going to cry. Michael had not been at all repentant. He had got what he wanted — they all moved on.

So You Think You Know About England?

1. Which castle is the seat of the Duke of Norfolk?
2. Which castle houses part of a university?
3. Which castle features a room with walls decorated by sea shells?
4. From which castle can no fewer than eight counties be seen?
5. Which is the largest castle in England?

Answers below.

5. *Windsor.*
4. *Beeston.*
3. *Skipton.*
2. *Durham.*
1. *Arundel.*

After that day, however, whenever Andy Hall was miserable or in trouble, they always knew where to find him. He would be down by the bridge staring at the pool and hoping against hope that the kingfisher would return.

YOU never ever saw it again?" Fiona repeated softly.

"Never," Andy said, then added: "Those were golden days, though, weren't they? What a happy childhood we had compared to some."

"Yes, there are a lot worse places than Kilbride, even if it isn't the most exciting town in the British Isles."

As she waved Andy away from the gate five minutes later, she thought how different the two brothers were — and had always been. Michael, clever, ambitious, anxious to be on the move. Andy, less brilliant, but more thoughtful, quite happy in his job with the town's only estate agent.

"Well?" Fiona's parents and Eileen came crowding into the hall anxious to hear about Michael.

"Very well, considering," she told them. "He looks fine, but he's maybe a wee bit edgy."

"No wonder, poor lad!" Mrs Boyd said.

"Yes! It was a sorry finish to his plans for a new life in Canada," Mr Boyd added sympathetically.

"He's probably thinking that, by right, you would have been out there with him now," Eileen pointed out. "Instead, he's had twelve months in and out of hospital."

A S Fiona prepared for bed that night her mind went back to the months before Michael's departure to Canada. What a shock it had been when he sprang the news on her!

To begin with she had been angry. They had been going out with each other for two years, and she had been dreadfully hurt that Michael had not taken her into his confidence. They had sat on a bench in the town-centre park and had a bitter quarrel.

Michael, she recalled, had sneered at her for having no ambition beyond being a dental receptionist. She had accused him of having no thought for anyone but himself.

They had made up only a week before Michael left for his new post with a firm of engineers in Toronto. How glad she had been that they had parted on good terms, when she had received news of Michael's accident.

And now?

Now she was determined to help him recover as quickly as possible. She would spend every evening with him. Walk with him up and down the road. Help him with his exercises.

With her head full of good intentions she ought to have felt happy as she finally lay down to sleep. But she didn't. Nor could she say why.

All she knew was that there was a tiny cloud settled obstinately on her horizon. She did not know where it had come from, but she had a feeling that, if she were not watchful it might gradually grow larger and larger . . .

On the Tuesday evening following Michael's arrival Fiona became aware of her sister watching her narrowly at suppertime. She was not surprised when there was a knock on her bedroom door later.

"You don't look too happy." Eileen came slowly into the room. "I didn't want to mention it in front of Mum and Dad . . . I just wondered . . . is Michael all right?"

"He's fine." Fiona's laugh sounded forced, even to her own ears.

"So why are you worrying?" Eileen asked, sitting down on the bed.

Fiona had been brushing her hair in front of the mirror. She smiled ruefully at her sister's reflection in the glass.

"You don't miss anything, do you?" She sighed, then added, "No. You're quite right. I can't pretend I'm very happy at the moment."

"And it's to do with Michael?"

Fiona dropped her head into her hands. She was not crying, but it was a gesture of despair.

"Oh, Eileen!" she said eventually. "It's all turned out so differently from what I expected. And no-one must know. That's the awful thing!"

"Know what? You can tell me, Fi! Surely?"

FIONA nodded. "It will be a relief to get it off my chest . . . I don't think I love Michael any more.

"I knew it from the moment I saw him again," she went on wretchedly. "I realise now I'd stopped loving him before he went away. But after I heard about his accident, I was so shocked and sorry that I forgot all those things about him that I didn't like. I invented a new Michael — if you see what I mean."

"But it's the old Michael who's come home." Eileen nodded, understanding immediately. She put her hand gently on her sister's shoulder. "So what are you going to do?"

"What can I do?" Fiona said bleakly. "I can't let him down in his condition. I'll just have to go on pretending."

"And if he asks you to marry him?"

"I daren't even think about that!"

Fiona was forced to think about it the very next evening.

Great-Grandmamma's Portrait

A PORTRAIT of Great-Grandmamma
  Hangs upon the wall,
Small, gilt-framed, and beautiful,
  And much admired by all.

Dark lashes trim, and wide, blue eyes
  That seem to follow me,
When busy at my tasks I go,
  She's smiling down at me.

But when at times in fretful mood
  I pass, with worried frown,
I feel she gently disapproves,
  Reproachful, looking down.

Whenever I feel lonely, sad,
  I sit and gaze awhile,
And find solace in her sweet face
  And Mona Lisa smile.

I look to her for guidance,
  She's my little voice within
All through the years, Great-Grandma, dear,
  My long-lost kith and kin.

Dorothy M. Loughran.

Andy had gone on to the tennis club after dropping Fiona at the Halls, and Mr and Mrs Hall were out visiting friends. Michael came hobbling round the side path, an uncharacteristically nervous smile on his face.

"Hello, Fi," he began quietly. "Would you like to come round to the patio and sit with me for a bit? There's something I have to say to you."

"My goodness!" Fiona exclaimed, trying to sound jocular. "You look as though it's going to take a lot of courage, whatever it is!"

"It is," Michael replied shortly as he led the way round to the back garden. "I've been trying to work round to it for three days now."

By the time they reached the seats on the patio, Fiona's heart was like lead. If Michael was working up to a proposal, as she suspected, what was she going to do? Give a downright refusal? Play for time?

The next second she received a shock that sent her head spinning.

"I've met someone else," Michael said abruptly. "I'm sorry, Fiona, but you have to know. Her name's Kerri Calder, and she nurses in the hospital where I was. As soon as I'm completely fit, I'm going back over to join her . . . I'm very, very sorry!"

Sheer relief made Fiona slump back in her seat. At the same time she realised that she must not look too overjoyed. That would do Michael's morale no good at all.

She managed to control her zooming spirits and say restrainedly, "I'm glad you've told me. And I wish you every happiness. Believe me."

"Thanks." Michael's voice was husky, and he stood up, obviously taking it for granted that Fiona would now want to leave. "Shall I phone for a taxi for you?" he asked gently.

"No," Fiona said. "I'll walk. It's a lovely evening."

She felt as though she were skimming a few inches above the sunlit pavements. It was a glorious June evening. Lawns were being mowed, children were playing in gardens . . .

THEN two youngsters passed her, carrying tennis racquets, and she was reminded of Andy. Suddenly she had a burning desire to find him; to tell him what had happened between Michael and herself.

She stopped walking and stood quite still for a few moments. The strength of her feeling made her quite breathless. Then she gave herself a little shake. She couldn't interrupt Andy in the middle of his game!

She would see him tomorrow probably. They had an unspoken arrangement to lunch together in a little restaurant midway between the dentist's surgery and Andy's office.

Fiona was humming a happy little tune as she finally walked through her own front door. Eileen was standing in the hall holding the telephone receiver.

"Michael," she whispered as Fiona hurried forward. "He sounds a bit worried."

Michael *was* worried.

"It's Andy," he explained. "We've had a row about our splitting up, Fiona. He seems to think I've treated you very badly. I did try to tell him that you understood and you'd taken it very well . . . You do understand don't you? I'm sorry, but those things just happen."

"Yes." Fiona frowned. "But what about Andy?"

"He got really upset," Michael said. "You know what he's like, if it's someone he cares about. And he obviously cares about you! He just flung out of the house twenty minutes ago. Walking. I wondered if he was coming up to you . . . If he does, try to calm him down, will you?"

"Yes! Of course I will," Fiona promised.

She went through to the kitchen to make herself a cup of tea and sat on her own drinking it. Poor Andy. He was so loyal and warm hearted. He would probably think she had been shattered by Michael's news.

Twenty minutes passed with no sign of him. Then the telephone rang again.

"Has he arrived?" Michael asked eagerly.

"No," she replied. "I'm afraid not."

"I hate stupid misunderstandings like this." Michael sighed. "Where can the idiot have gone to?"

"Don't worry, I have an idea," Fiona said slowly. "I'll phone you back in an hour. If Andy's not home by then, I think I'll have found him."

The Good Samaritan

LIFE had hurt me very much,
  Unhappiness did hound me,
And my tide of sorrows rose so high,
  I thought they would have drowned
    me.
And then a good Samaritan —
  A friend came in and found me.
She did not speak of all the ills
  And sorrows that had downed me.
Oh, by her loving kindness
  She hath forever bound me —
For she gave me what I needed most —
  She put her arms around me!

Miriam Eker.

THERE had been a lot of building along Waterworks Road in the past 14 years. She had to walk a fair distance before she left the houses behind.

The Old Brig had not been altered in any way, though. And the pool still lay below it, greeny-black and mysterious.

"Andy!" Fiona called, quickening her step.

She saw him start, as he turned to face her. His clear, grey eyes were wide with anxiety.

"Oh, Fiona," he began hoarsely. "I'm so sorry for what's happened. I'll never forgive Michael for doing this to you. Never! I just don't understand him. Why can't he see what he's throwing away?"

Fiona leaned back against the parapet of the bridge and took Andy's hand in her own.

"Listen to me," she said quietly. "I want to explain something to you."

She talked for a long time, calmly, and with a growing sense of relief. When she had finished she looked at Andy, waiting for his reaction.

The red deepened in his cheeks as he looked down into her eyes. "I ought to feel sorry about this, but somehow I can't. To tell you the truth, I feel almost happy. What a rotten brother I am. And what a rotten friend!" He bit his lip and turned away.

"A rotten friend!" Fiona exclaimed indignantly. "Andy Hall! What are you talking about?"

She was still holding his hand and now she shook it a little. "Maybe I have been living in a silly dream world for the past year," she began. "But one thing I know was real, and that was your kindness. You've become the closest friend I have.

"I love being with you. I like the way you care about people . . . your sense of humour . . . the way you always rush to help any lame dog in sight . . . so I can't listen to you saying such things about yourself!"

She looked up at him and saw him draw his breath in sharply. He disengaged his hand and put an arm around her shoulder.

"Do you remember that day when we saw the kingfisher?" he asked quietly.

She nodded.

"It made such an impression on me," Andy went on. "I was too young to even try to put it into words, but everything about it seemed magical. I remember standing here and staring at it and wishing it would sit there for ever. I thought I'd never felt as happy in my life before. It was like one of my fairy stories come true."

"Then Michael brought it to an end," Fiona remarked wryly.

"Yes," Andy said. "But now, after all these years, he's the one who's brought the magic back to me."

Fiona looked up at him and saw the love in his eyes.

"What do you mean?" She smiled, knowing all the time, but wanting to hear it from Andy's lips.

"I love you very, very much," Andy said quietly. "And I thought I would never be able to let you know. Even when I thought you loved Michael I was happy just to help you."

"Which is precisely why I love you very, very much, too." Fiona sighed, drawing Andy close.

They kissed gently in the twilight, just as the light evening breeze sent a ripple across the green surface of the Kingfisher Pool. □

BUCKIE

Buckie is the largest town in the old county of Banffshire. Until the decline of the herring industry, it was one of the most important fishing ports in Britain, but these days it is a favourite for holidaymakers. There is plenty for them to see, including the Buckie Maritime Museum, and golfers have the choice of two courses. Visitors with a car at their disposal have access to a variety of splendid coastal scenery, or can opt for the mountain grandeur of the Cairngorms, including the famous Whisky Trail, if they feel so inclined.

BUCKIE, BANFFSHIRE

Man To Man

by KATE HANNAH

AS young Mr Rutledge, of Oliver Rutledge & Sons, stood in the arcade of the family department store, his mind was far away. It was not like him at all, completely out of character. Perhaps that was why he made the mistake.

Rutledge & Sons was one of the smaller departmental stores in the city, priding itself upon exclusiveness. Discerning customers who came through the ornate swing doors could always be assured of careful service, for Rutledge's motto was well known throughout the city: *Keep a customer happy and you keep a customer.*

Young Mister Fergus, as departmental heads would call him, had been brought up in the trade. An only son, he would go on to succeed his father, and grandfather, who had begun the successful family store. His father, Oliver, had started Fergus in the basement and taught him everything he knew.

Just like his father, Mister Fergus wasn't given to sentiment and, to be absolutely honest, didn't possess a particularly generous nature — well, at least not to his hard-working staff, who stood in awe of him most of the time.

Mister Fergus, just like his

father before him, believed in a hard day's work for a reasonable pay, but at Christmastime, a bonus was paid to compensate for all the extra hours the staff were asked to work.

This year, Rutledge's were celebrating a very special anniversary. It was 50 years since they had moved into the popular city site and Oliver had asked his son to come up with something special this year with regard to their Christmas display in the arcade leading up to the front doors.

Money was not to be spared — within reason — and Fergus had surpassed himself. The animated Nativity scene was catching the imagination of every passerby. Mister Fergus was feeling justly proud of his achievement and couldn't wait to take Myra down to see it.

Mister Fergus had married Myra Goodchild just over a year ago. Mister Fergus, although known as *young* Mr Rutledge, was nearing 40, and when he fell in love and married Myra, Oliver and his wife Maidie had expressed just a little disappointment. They loved Myra, of course, with her steady brown eyes and even temperament, but she was a bit on the young side and not in the least store-orientated.

Myra had studied sociology at university, sported CND badges and talked earnestly about the cause of peace for her brother man. Myra, in their eyes, was just a bit of a rebel, but Fergus adored her, and they felt sure that she would soon settle down.

It was when Fergus took his father down to see the display that the first doubt crept in.

"Absolutely splendid, my boy. You've done the firm proud. Where on earth did you get all those figures?"

Fergus explained how he had enlisted the help of the city art school and he'd commissioned a firm of electricians to wire the lot up. Every figure in the display was animated, even the little sheep on the hill who walked on stalky woolly legs, following the star to Bethlehem.

"Really eye-catching, my boy," his father enthused once more, then stroked his chin thoughtfully. "But tell me, Fergus, do the shepherds or the wise men arrive first?"

Fergus wrinkled his brow.

"Do you know, Father, I'm really not sure about that."

To be absolutely honest, he wasn't a churchgoing man. Most Sundays he had to come in and go over the week's trading figures, now Father was semi-retired. Still, he could easily check up with Myra tonight. Myra sang in the cathedral choir and was an expert on such matters.

The animated Nativity scene had been something of a mechanical miracle, each figure moving along a complicated series of wires which were cunningly hidden behind tinsel. Angels really flew above the cave, their gilt wings catching the lights trained upon them, and Joseph would indicate with his staff as he welcomed each new visitor to the stable.

THE LOMONDS IN FEBRUARY

BEN LOMOND reigns in splendour
O'er the Loch of high renown.
Upon his cairn and lower slopes
   Pure snow falls gently down.
The February sunshine
   Glints powerful and bright
Upon majestic summit high,
   And clothes him all in light.

Though it were but the snowdrops
   month
   The Loch — she gently danced
Rippling against her bonnie shores
   While I stood there entranced.
My mind enshrines you, bonnie loch
   Wher'ever I shall stray,
Remembering your lovely self
   On a February day.

           Sister M. Mannes.

It was really putting the seal on the superb sales campaign, for already customers were pouring into the arcade just to look at the display, and at almost any time you could guarantee a line of children with their noses pressed against the plate-glass windows.

MISTER FERGUS bade his father goodbye and watched the stooped figure climb into the chauffeur-driven limousine which sped off towards the airport. His mum and dad would be spending this Christmas in Portugal where the family owned a villa.

He had suggested to Myra that they might join his parents, but she had looked shocked and was obviously very disappointed at the idea.

They had just recently moved into a brand-new bungalow and Myra wanted to spend Christmas in it.

"Christmas together, Fergus," she had chided him, "in our very own home. How could you think otherwise?"

And of course, Fergus could deny her nothing, not after he'd heard her exciting news that at last she was pregnant. There was going to be yet another Rutledge to carry on the firm's good name.

WELL, now Father was off, it was time for his morning cuppa. Young Mr Rutledge was about to head for the lift when he heard a young voice raised.

"Look, Ma. Look what some idiot's done here. Got the wise men going into the stable before the shepherds."

Fergus Rutledge spun round and saw a boy in a shabby anorak with his nose pressed hard against the glass. He was pulling at his mother's arm.

"Anyone knows the shepherds were the first to see the star."

The woman looked closer.

"Why, Patrick, you're right. Do you know, son, I'd never noticed that before, and I've passed it every day this week. Now fancy Mr Rutledge making a mistake like that."

The woman was wearing a rather faded red coat and, as she turned quickly, discovered that she was being stared at by a man with a deep frown on his face.

Fergus Rutledge transferred his attention to the boy now.

"Are you quite sure about that?" he demanded irritably, and the boy grinned up at him.

" 'Course I'm sure. At home we always hide our wise men behind the crib until it's their time to go in. Isn't that right, Ma?"

The woman bit her lip.

"Y-yes, Patrick, but it's really none of our business, dear."

Drat the boy, Fergus thought irritably. It would mean disconnecting all those wires and rearranging the figures. A nuisance, of course, but it would have to be done. In young Mr Rutledge's book, perfection in all things was desirable, even when it came to shepherds and wise men.

There was something familiar about the woman's face, he decided, although for the life of him he couldn't see where he could have met her before. She'd said something about passing the display each morning, but she couldn't possibly be a sales assistant. He would never have employed anyone who looked as shabby as that.

"Excuse me, madam," he asked now, "but do I know you from somewhere?"

The woman's drawn face grew pale.

"I work in the kitchen of your restaurant, sir."

Then it came to him in a flash. Mister Fergus prided himself upon an excellent memory and he never forgot a face.

He had gone up to the fifth floor to check with the head waiter about the festive menu being offered to customers and had overheard a heated conversation coming from the kitchen. It had gone something like this.

"But I've never asked for time off before, Mr Brown, and this is important. You must see that?"

Why the conversation had made an impression was because of Mr Brown, the head waiter's reply.

"Time off during Christmas week, Mrs O'Flynn. You know that's impossible. The restaurant will be mobbed all week. I can't spare anyone. You'll just have to get your husband to stand in for you. The firm comes first."

The head waiter had been with the firm for 30 years and was a trusted employee. The man's reprimand had been fully justified and gained his boss's approval. He had just glanced into the kitchen to see the culprit and caught sight of this pale-looking woman with a fuzz of hair which might once have been blonde.

No doubt the woman had been trying to get a few extra days' holiday at Christmas.

Now, as he studied the woman's face again, he noticed drawn lines about the old-young face. The boy also looked rather wan and when he turned away with his mother, limped rather badly.

"Just one moment, please."

The woman spun round.

"S-sir, I'm not due to start my shift until eleven. I was just showing Patrick the display."

Suddenly Fergus Rutledge experienced a qualm of guilt.

"Mrs O'Flynn, isn't it?"

She nodded her head desolately.

"I'd like you to take your son and come with me please?"

The Question

DOES Santa Claus exist, Dad?
　　The boys at school say no.
They say he's just a childish myth
　　Invented long ago.
I'm getting pretty big now,
　　That's why I'm asking you,
Because it is important
　　To know which things are true.

You've put the matter squarely,
　　I'm glad, my lad, because
You're old enough to understand
　　The truth of Santa Claus.
Now, would you say that kindness
　　And generosity
Exist within the world today
　　For all of us to see?

If you are sure of these things
　　The truth you have not missed
And you will understand the way
　　Santa *does* exist!

Gay Wilson.

FERGUS RUTLEDGE swept the pair of them along the arcade, in through the swing doors and into the private lift which was reserved for management and which carried them to his top-floor office.

"What's your name, boy?" he asked as he pulled a chair out for Mrs O'Flynn and waited until she sat down.

Man To Man

"Patrick," the boy said evenly, not one sign of fear on his face, at least.

"Well, Patrick, do you like mincemeat pies?"

"Not half."

He ordered tea and the speciality of the house for all, then telephoned the shop's electrician and window dresser, giving instructions for the alteration to the Nativity scene. Sitting back in his executive black leather chair, he studied the woman closely.

"Now I'd like you to tell me, Mrs O'Flynn, why you wanted time off from work this week."

The woman was speechless and it was Patrick again who acted as spokesman.

"She wanted to move in with me when I go to the infirmary this afternoon. They allow mothers to stay overnight, you see."

Mrs O'Flynn seemed to have regained her poise.

"Yes, Mr Rutledge, you see, Patrick's name has been down for surgery for over two years and it would have to be now that his turn has come up. We're hoping he'll be out just before Christmas, but there's no guarantee."

"I don't mind a bit if I have to stay in, Ma. You know that."

The boy's face was filled with compassion. It seemed that the mother was more upset than he.

"I've waited long enough for this, Ma. There will be other Christmases."

Patrick went on to explain that the operation was to straighten his leg which had been crooked since a car accident at the age of three. If the operation was successful he might even play football, he added.

"Couldn't your father have taken some time off?" Fergus asked.

"Yes," the boy told him. "But he's just landed a job after being unemployed for five years. He doesn't want to take any chances."

F ERGUS RUTLEDGE suddenly thought of something. Myra would have loved young Patrick. He was a brave lad, obviously without one drop of false sentiment in him. A boy who wouldn't want his father to risk his new job just to be with him in hospital when he went through his vital operation.

As for the mother, she had been denied leave of absence because Rutledge & Sons were having a bumper festive season and couldn't spare the staff.

Mary O'Flynn was glancing anxiously towards the clock.

"I'll have to be going soon, Mr Rutledge. I start work in five minutes."

It was at that moment that young Mr Rutledge broke with tradition; broke his own rules as he put it later to Myra. He lifted the telephone and asked for Tom Brown, the head waiter, to come to his office immediately.

"Now look, Tom, I want you to do something for me."

"Yes, sir. Of course, sir."

"I want you to find a temporary replacement for Mrs O'Flynn here,

83

over the Christmas week. You see, she has to go into hospital with young Patrick here. It's a very special case, Tom, and I'm relying on you to do your utmost."

One did not argue with young Mr Rutledge, and Tom Brown nodded his head wisely, but sent a strange look in Mary O'Flynn's direction, just the same.

"I'll get on to the Labour Exchange straightaway, sir," he assured his employer.

"That's a good man," Fergus said approvingly and turned to offer young Patrick another mincemeat pie.

The problem had been solved easily and Fergus Rutledge felt suffused by a sense of well-being. He knew that Myra, at least, would approve his action.

T HE sense of well-being lasted until they left the canteen and walked downstairs to the toy department. Well, after all, the boy had saved the firm's good name, drawing his attention to the mistake in the window display.

"Anything you like, Patrick," he said extravagantly.

The boy's eyes were like saucers. There were computerised toys, bicycles, model train sets.

"Could I have a harmonica, mister? I've always wanted one of those," he confessed.

As he said to Myra later, it had been such a modest request, but Mrs O'Flynn assured him that Patrick had a way with musical instruments, and to prove it, the boy had given them a rendering of *She'll Be Coming Round The Mountain*, right there in the toy department.

Myra was looking particularly beautiful tonight, he thought. Pregnancy had added yet another dimension to his adorable wife's charm.

If she were to give him a son who grew up just like Patrick O'Flynn, full of courage and with such a sense of purpose, then he would be more than happy.

Perhaps it was just a flash in the pan. Perhaps he would never behave in such a generous fashion again, offering a boy the pick of his toy department. After all, Rutledge & Sons was not a charitable institution.

But then, it wasn't every Christmas that one's wife could say that all their wishes were to come true at last. Their child wouldn't be born in a draughty stable, but would arrive in summer when the sun was high in the sky. Yes, right in the middle of the summer sales. How typical of a Rutledge!

Still it was the best Christmas he would ever spend, at home in their new house with Myra in his arms each night, sharing dreams for the future.

And it was going to be the best Christmas, too, for Patrick O'Flynn, or so he told his mother as they walked the long road leading up to the infirmary, whether he spent it in hospital or at home.

Patrick was carrying his case in one hand and in the other he clasped his harmonica. ☐

THEN HIS EYES WERE OPENED

by Elsie Jackson

"COMING for a coffee?" Laura Douglas asked as she paused on the library steps to push her hair out of her eyes.

"Why not?" Behind his spectacles Dave Kilbride's eyes twinkled good-humouredly. "It's too late now to read all those books the professor recommended!"

"Yes." Red-headed Cathy Brown sighed. "I'm so strung-up, I'd never be able to concentrate, anyway. It seems so unreal. Finals tomorrow!"

"What about you, Colin?" Laura asked a broad-shouldered young man who was standing on the step above her. "Can we tempt you away from your last-minute swotting?"

Colin laid his hand lightly on Laura's shoulder. "Afraid I can't," he said regretfully. "Jill's come up to town specially to treat me to a meal . . . In fact, there she is! I'd better go." He gave Laura's shoulder a gentle squeeze as he left, and she felt her cheeks redden.

"Oh, no! Look at that clown!" Cathy exclaimed suddenly with a hoot of laughter.

Laura, looking in the direction of her pointing finger, saw Dave halfway down the avenue doing his Groucho Marx walk, oblivious of the amused glances of the passers-by.

"Eve-of-examination madness." Laura laughed, then she suddenly became serious. "Oh, I'm going to miss you all when we go our separate ways."

"And some more than others!" Cathy commented with a sly glance at her friend.

"What do you mean?"

"I mean Colin."

"Colin? Why should I miss him more than the rest of you?" Laura asked curtly as they started after Dave.

"Oh, Laura!" Cathy said impatiently. "I'm not blind. I've caught you looking at him when he was deep in his books, or walking across the quad . . . and the expression in your eyes!"

Laura's cheeks flamed. "Don't be silly, Cathy. Colin has a steady girlfriend. He and Jill have been going about together since they were fourteen. He might as well be married!"

"In that case, why does he make sheep's eyes at you, when you're not watching?" Cathy asked with a short laugh.

"He does not! Does he?" Laura asked, unable to keep the tense little note of hope out of her voice.

But before Cathy could answer her, they had caught up with Dave. He put an arm round both their shoulders and swept them along, protesting laughingly, to the college coffee shop.

THAT evening, though, when she was alone in her small bedsitter, trying to concentrate on her last-minute revision, Laura's mind kept going back to what Cathy had said.

She had known Colin McKenzie for four years now. It had only been during the last two, however, that she had been aware of a gradual change in her feelings towards him.

Of the original English class of 20, only four had decided to attempt an Honours degree. And naturally they had come to know one another fairly well.

Over an occasional coffee, or sitting alone with him in the library, Laura had learned a lot about Colin's background. He'd lost both his parents when he was four years old and had been brought up by grandparents in a small Lanarkshire town.

It was his schoolteachers who had pressed for him to go to university, and apparently his grandparents had taken a lot of persuasion. This was why he had been a constant hard worker, determined to show his gratitude for the chance he had been given.

Once he had mentioned the fact that when he was a child there had never been a single book in the house. And Laura had thought how different her own upbringing had been, with two schoolteacher parents and every room spilling over with books.

It was from that moment that a tenderness for Colin had started. And that tenderness had grown. Liftings of the heart if she met him unexpectedly in the common-room, or walking through the park . . . a warm glow, when his grey eyes met hers as they shared a joke . . .

But, of course, there was always Jill to be considered. Jill Ross, the girl-back-home, who lived only three doors away from Colin's grandparents. Jill, who came up to town occasionally to go out for a meal with Colin, or to bring him his birthday presents, or to go to the cinema with him.

Laura had seen her only from a distance, a tall, dark, confident-looking girl. She had obviously not been anxious to meet Colin's friends, for they had invited her to come for coffee with them on three occasions and been refused. Colin had said that she was shy.

So what was the point in sitting daydreaming about Colin McKenzie? He was "spoken for" to use a good, old-fashioned phrase. And yet . . . what had Cathy meant? Did Colin really make "sheep's eyes" at her? What a dreadful expression!

Laura shook herself. This would not do! A milestone in her life was coming up tomorrow, and here she was wasting her time. She resolutely drew her thick, green Shakespeare folder towards her and settled down to work.

THE examinations lasted for eight days. Inevitably a heatwave arrived with the first of them, so that despite wide-open windows in the examination halls, palms became sweaty and throats dry.

"Never mind. Not long to go now," they told one another bravely, as they staggered home at the end of each day.

Laura, Dave and Cathy phoned their parents each night to report on the day's paper. Colin's grandparents did not have a telephone.

"Anyway they wouldn't understand what I was talking about." He smiled.

Then, finally, the last day came. The last paper. The last question.

Dave Kilbride stood in the quadrangle shaking his head. "I can't believe it," he was saying. "I just can't believe it!"

"Cheer up!" Kathy said, chuckling. "The worst is yet to come. When do we get our results?"

"The best is yet to come!" Colin smiled at Laura. "The thought of our celebration dinner kept me going all afternoon."

"Oh, yes!" Laura sighed. "Let's go and get dressed up, Cathy. We'll make this an evening to remember."

Her words came back to her at eleven o'clock that night as she strolled home with Colin through the park. It had seemed only sensible that he should offer to take her home, since his own flat was in the same area.

Then, somehow, as they talked, Laura found Colin's arm round her waist. That seemed right, too. And nothing could have seemed more right than the magic moment when he finally held her and kissed her.

"I've wanted to do that for so long!" he whispered.

I'll never be happier than at this moment. Never! Laura told herself, as she held Colin close.

I KNEW it! I told you!" Cathy said triumphantly next morning, as she sat in Laura's flat having a cup of coffee. Having finished her own packing, she had come round to help with Laura's, and Laura had been unable to keep her happiness to herself.

"So where do you go from here?" Cathy asked, her eyes twinkling at her friend's radiant face.

"He's going to write," Laura said. "And he's going to try to meet me a couple of times before the twenty-sixth."

June 26 was the day the examination results were to be pinned up on the notice board. It was three weeks away, and the four friends were all going home for a well-earned rest in the meanwhile.

"And then?" Cathy pursued.

"Oh, Cathy! How do I know?" Laura laughed. "It's all happened so unexpectedly."

"He'll have to tell Jill," Cathy pointed out.

Laura flushed. "It's not as if they were engaged, or anything," she said. "I mean, it won't be all that difficult."

"Well, I'm going to phone you at least twice a week," Cathy threatened. "Then you can tell me all the latest developments."

"Nosey!" Laura exclaimed in feigned indignation.

"No, I'm not!" Cathy protested. "I'm just interested. We did promise we would be each other's bridesmaids, so I must be prepared."

However, as the days passed, and there was still no word from Colin, Laura's happiness dimmed a little.

By the end of a week, she had written him two long letters but had had no reply. She began to think he might have fallen ill, and started to worry. If only he was on the telephone, she fretted.

By the end of 10 days, and with another letter still unanswered, she was beginning to feel desperate.

She had not realised just how deep her feelings for Colin were. She found herself aching for the sight of him and the sound of his voice.

When Cathy phoned for the second time to ask how the romance was progressing, Laura spilled all her unhappiness out.

"Why not go down to his home and see what's happened?" Cathy suggested. "It's only two bus journeys, after all. He doesn't live on the other side of the country."

"Do you think I should?" Laura asked uncertainly. "It seems so . . ."

"Oh, for goodness' sake, we're not living in Victorian times. Girls can take the initiative nowadays, if need be."

"Yes, you're right. I'll go to Townbridge tomorrow."

By leaving home at eleven o'clock Laura was able to reach Townbridge just before three in the afternoon. She had Colin's address firmly engraved on her mind and asked directions at the bus station. She braced herself and nervously set off on her mission.

After a 10-minute walk, she found herself in a housing scheme where she began to recognise landmarks from Colin's conversation. There was the school he'd attended as a little boy. There was the park where he'd fallen from the chute. And here was Dornoch Crescent!

Her heart was beating wildly by the time she reached the gate of number 33. She felt as though she had not seen Colin for 10 years, far less 10 days!

What if he's not at home, she thought suddenly as she rang the doorbell. But a moment later her fears vanished. It was Colin, himself, book in hand, who answered the door.

"LAURA!" he exclaimed, turning bright red.

He did not appear to be happy to see her. In fact, he looked both embarrassed and shocked.

"I wondered what had happened to you, Colin." She faltered. "No letter after all this time . . ."

"You haven't got my letter, then?" he asked, staring at her in perplexity.

"No, silly!" she said, trying to make light of the situation, and attempting a laugh. "I've come because I haven't had a letter!"

Colin swallowed hard. "You'd better come in, Laura," he mumbled, with a faint smile. "You've had a long journey."

He ushered her into an old-fashioned, rather dark living-room, where an old lady was sitting knitting by the window.

So You Think You Know About Wales?

1. Where is the island of Skokholm?
2. Where was the investiture of Prince Charles as Prince of Wales held?
3. Which city is the smallest cathedral city in Britain?
4. Where was the wizard Merlin alleged to have been born?
5. How many counties can be seen from Pen y Fan, the summit of the Brecon Beacons?

Answers below.

1. *Milford Haven.*
2. *Caernarvon Castle.*
3. *St David's.*
4. *Carmarthen.*
5. *14.*

"Gran," he said awkwardly. "This is Laura Douglas. She's in my class at university, and she's come down to see me."

"That's nice," old Mrs McKenzie said politely, nodding at Laura. "I should think she'd like a cup of tea, then. Do sit down, dear," she added.

As Laura perched on the end of the settee, Colin said, "I'll just see if Grandpa would like a cup, too. He's down at the bottom of the garden."

Laura had never felt more uncomfortable in her life. She was sure there had been an expression of relief on Colin's face at the chance of escaping even for a few minutes. And Mrs McKenzie was obviously becoming more ill at ease with every passing moment.

When Colin returned with his grandfather there was a renewed flurry of embarrassment. Resentment, almost, because the old man had been disturbed at his weeding and dragged in to join the company.

No-one can even bear to look at me, Laura thought wretchedly. They all prefer the blessed carpet!

"Coo-ee! Anyone at home?" The voice came from the kitchen, and a moment later Jill Ross came breezing in, carrying a loaded shopping bag.

IMMEDIATELY the atmosphere improved. Mrs McKenzie beamed, and her husband strode over to relieve Jill of the bag.

"We've got a visitor," he told the young woman unnecessarily, since she was staring curiously at Laura. "One of Colin's classmates from the college."

"Oh, gosh!" Jill laughed. "One of the Brainy Brigade."

Colin introduced Laura briefly, and Jill headed back for the kitchen. "I suppose I'd better make the tea, then," she called easily. "If we wait for Colin, we'll be dying of thirst."

"It's well seen you know him!" Colin's grandmother laughed.

He hasn't told her! She doesn't know!

The realisation hit Laura like a physical blow. She sat in stunned silence, trying to respond with a smile or a nod to the odd remark which was thrown her way.

Jill handed her her tea. "So what brought you down here, Laura?" she asked casually.

"Oh, it was just a book I wanted to borrow," she blurted out eventually.

"Oh, you're not another book addict, like Colin, are you?" Jill said with an exaggerated sigh. "He wastes hours that way!"

"Yes. You'll have to put your foot down once you're married, Jill." Mr McKenzie chuckled. "Otherwise you'll have to do all the gardening and decorating yourself."

Laura looked at Colin, but he refused to meet her eyes. As soon as she could, she stood up and said she must go.

"Don't forget your book," Jill reminded her.

"No," Colin muttered. "I'll fetch it."

He dived into his room, and came back with a book, which he thrust into Laura's hand. She knew he must have picked it at random from his bookshelves and when she looked down at it she almost laughed aloud. It was Milton's "Paradise Lost."

Colin and Jill both came to the door with her.

"Thank you for the tea," she said, politely, as a visitor should.

Then His Eyes Were Opened

"I expect your letter will arrive tomorrow," Colin said in a small, tight voice. "The one you've been worrying about."

"Yes, I expect so." Laura had to turn her head away and look along the street to hide the tears that were forming, despite herself.

By the time she reached the bus station, the inclination to weep had gone, but the dead, cold weight on her heart was frightening.

How could Colin have done this to her? For a terrible five minutes she hated him with a black, unforgiving anger.

Then she remembered him, as she had seen him last, standing miserably at the door. She knew that she still loved him, in spite of everything. And that the pain would not go away for a long, long time.

IT was a long letter, which said the same thing over again and again with variations. Colin had made a mistake. He was more sorry about it than he could say. He and Jill would be getting engaged after the results came out.

Why had it all happened? Laura asked herself that question repeatedly as she sat moping in her room. It had spoiled everything. She'd always thought she'd remember those last lovely two years with special affection. Now there would always be a shadow.

The phone rang one afternoon and her heart leapt stupidly as she rushed to answer it. It turned out to be Dave with the news that he had landed a job in Hong Kong.

"Hong Kong!" Laura exclaimed in dismay. "Oh, Dave! We'll never see you again!"

"You should be so lucky!" he quipped.

As she hung the receiver up, she realised that she was going to miss him very much indeed. Warm-hearted Dave, with his clowning and his nonsense, was very dear to her. She trailed back upstairs feeling more depressed than ever.

Inevitably June 26 arrived. Laura saw Dave give her a sharp look as she joined him in front of the notice board at three o'clock.

"Cheer up," he said comfortingly. "I'm sure you'll do well."

"Last-minute jitters," she said truthfully — though it was the thought of having to face Colin again, rather than her exam results, that was worrying her.

Cathy came running up to stand beside them. Laura had given her a brief account of the disastrous end of her romance on the phone, so Cathy asked no questions, but gave her friend's arm a comforting squeeze.

"Here's Colin!" Dave announced suddenly. "Just in time, too! Mr Goldson's coming right behind him with the results."

It was a fortunate coincidence, for in the resultant flurry of apprehension and excitement, Laura had no need to look at Colin. Her eyes were firmly directed towards the all-important notice board. There was a moment's breathless silence, then a communal sigh of relief. Everyone had made it!

"Come on!" Dave called, giving a wild whoop. "What are we waiting for? Celebration-time! Coffee and chocolate cake! And something a bit more elaborate later on! We'll have an evening we'll remember."

"I'm sorry," Laura said quickly. "I can't. I'm meeting someone."

"You can't be!" Dave protested indignantly. "You can't desert your best friends in their hour of triumph."

"Sorry," Laura repeated, feeling her cheeks hot. "I really must go. Congratulations, everyone." She still had not looked at Colin.

As she started away from the group, she heard Dave give a final, hurt: "But, Laura —" Then Cathy said something and he fell silent.

She walked quickly to the main university gates, tears beginning to prick at her eyes. Oh, why has it all ended like this? Why?

Someone was running up behind her, and she frowned in exasperation. If only Dave would leave her alone!

It wasn't Dave's voice. It was Colin's.

"Laura. Can we talk?"

He was by her side, and she looked away from him.

"There's no need," she said tightly. "I got the message. You spelled it out very clearly."

"Please, listen!" he said urgently. "I made a mistake."

"You told me!" she said angrily. "And I accept it, so, for heaven's sake, don't go on about it! It's been painful enough!"

"That's not what I mean!" he said desperately, his voice breaking a little. "Give me a chance to explain, even if you won't forgive me."

She turned to look at him, and at the sight of his pained face her heart contracted. She still felt the same way about him, despite all that had happened. She could not bear to see him look so miserable.

"All right," she said finally. "But we can't talk here. Let's go down to the park."

THEY walked in silence and Laura made for a quiet corner near the pond.

"Come on, then." She sighed, sitting down on an empty bench. "I'm listening."

"I must explain about Jill and me . . ." he began hoarsely.

If only he knew how that phrase "Jill and me" hurt, Laura thought wretchedly.

She nodded silently, and gave Colin a wan smile.

"She sort of took me over when we were in the third form at school," Colin went on. "I was glad of it, too. It was lonely for me at home, with just Gran and Grandpa, and I never had much pocket money to go out with the gang. Her parents took me on outings with them. I became like one of the family, I suppose . . ."

"That was good," Laura said quietly, thinking of the lonely little boy he had once been.

"We've never really looked in any other direction," Colin went on hesitantly. "Everyone took it for granted that, when I'd finished at university, I'd come back and marry Jill."

I know all this! Laura wanted to scream. Why do you keep rubbing it in?

"I suppose I knew that I was changing, growing into a different person," Colin went on. "Jill was still happy doing the same old things every weekend — cinema, disco, visiting her aunts and uncles — but I needed more than that. I wanted to discuss books with her, to go to the theatre . . . I was already restless when you came into my life, Laura, and gradually I knew I was falling in love with you. You were so warm, and lively, and so very, very pretty!

"And yet I couldn't bring myself to cause unhappiness at home. After all, it wasn't Jill's fault that so much about me had changed — my way of life, my interests, my friends.

"In addition, I knew what a blow it would be to Gran and Grandpa if I were to dash their hopes for Jill and me. They'd watched us grow up together.

"I wasn't very good at chatting up girls. I suppose because Jill was nearly always with me at discos and so on in Townbridge, I didn't have to take my courage in my hands like the other lads when they met girls."

As he paused, Laura remembered her own carefree teenage years. She'd been lucky, she realised, always to be part of an easy-going, sociable crowd. Not only that, although she'd worked hard at her studies, she'd enjoyed the social side of university life. She'd never known the agonies of shyness or of being a wallflower.

With a pang, she admitted to herself that until she'd met Colin, she'd never lost her heart to anyone.

Colin stood up and paced back and forward in front

THE VISIT

FRESH roses in her room. Their sheen will last for days and their fragrance stay all week.

Did you bring these roses when you spent an hour with this lonely old soul? Give her your news? She will savour your words for days ahead. Show her snaps of your grand-children in Toronto? All week now she'll recall your daughter as a child long ago.

You stayed one hour — it will grow into many hours of pleasure for her.

You brought her roses. Their fragrance will fill her room for many days. But you also brought yourself. The fragrance of your presence will fill her life with a sweetness for as long as the roses will last.

Rev. T. R. S. Campbell.

of the park bench, his hands in his pockets, shaking his head. He stopped in front of Laura and looked her straight in the eye.

"Yet I realised I was looking forward more and more to the times when I would meet you, Laura. At first I began to watch for you in class. Then when we started going for coffee in a group, I appreciated that it was part of university life I'd neglected in the past. With Dave there, I could sit and listen, and learn what it was like to talk about things other than neighbours and what was happening in Townbridge.

"Most of all, though, I enjoyed working beside you in the library.

There was a kind of warmth knowing that we had the same aims."

I'll have to run, if he keeps on, Laura thought desperately. He's breaking my heart!

"We talked the same language, too," Colin went on. "I couldn't believe it, that night after our dinner, when I found out you cared for me, too."

Laura could keep silent no longer. "Much good it did me!" she cried bitterly. "You decided you'd made a mistake and that your place was with Jill after all! That's what you're going to tell me, now, isn't it? That I helped to bring you close to Jill again."

Colin reached out for her hand, his head bowed.

"No," he said. "I'm going to tell you what a despicable coward I've been.

"When I went home after the exams I'd every intention of telling Jill about you. Then when the moment came, I realised just what a commotion it was going to cause with my own family — and hers. I just couldn't face it.

"Instead I kidded myself along. I told myself I'd been wrong to become involved with you and that I'd betrayed Jill. I shut my eyes to the truth, until you arrived on our doorstep. Then I couldn't fool myself any longer. Do you despise me? I wouldn't blame you for a moment if you did."

"No," Laura whispered.

"I've told Jill everything," he went on. "She's upset, but I think she'll see eventually that it was all for the best. I would have been doing her a terrible wrong, marrying her and knowing I didn't really love her."

"Has there been a commotion?" Laura asked anxiously.

"I'm afraid so," Colin replied ruefully. "I'm not a very popular lad in Townbridge at the moment."

"Oh, darling! I am sorry!"

Colin looked up sharply. "Does that mean I'm forgiven?" he asked.

"I've never stopped loving you. Not for a moment," Laura said simply.

They kissed. Then Colin pulled her gently to her feet.

"Let's go and find Dave and Cathy," he said. "I think we should tell them there's another reason to celebrate. Don't you?" □

WELLINGTON SQUARE, AYR

A busy area in a busy town, Wellington Square houses the County Buildings, Court House and a monument to a son of Ayr whose name is a household word — John McAdam, the road builder, was born in Ayr in 1756. Ayr, of course, was praised by Robert Burns in "Tam o' Shanter" as being unsurpassed "for honest men and bonnie lasses." Today it is a centre for people from the surrounding countryside, and in addition is a very popular holiday destination. With a beautiful, extensive beach, three golf-courses and a racecourse, it is no wonder that holidaymakers return time and again.

WELLINGTON SQUARE, AYR

I LAY, face down, on a lounger in the Tenerife sunshine, drowsy with heat and sun, my oiled limbs turning at last to a delicate brown, after a week of Aunt Chrissie's ministrations. Lazily, I watched the swimmers at the pool through half-open eyes. Then I blinked, suddenly awake. It was him!

No! It couldn't be! Not him — the man who by accidentally flicking cigar ash down my best white skirt had broken my run of bad luck. Couldn't be . . . yes, it was him!

Our chance meeting happened nine months ago, on a fine golden September day in Glasgow. I was more than a little depressed, being about to attend my twenty-fifth job interview, since graduating as Bachelor of Education. Now I had given up trying solely for teaching jobs. This advert asked for a personable, educated person, competent and able to type, for a university professor. I had no idea what it entailed, but the salary offered was excellent, and I was desperate, even beginning to doubt my own abilities. But I did have an "O"-level in business studies and was used to doing my father's farming returns.

The bus to Glasgow from Ayrshire was delayed, and I'd tried to find the house in the West End. But now I was lost. The only solution was to get a taxi. When a cab rolled to a stop at the kerb beside me just then, it was almost too good to be true. The door opened and a happy-looking, tall young man got out, a large bouquet of flowers in one hand and a huge cigar in the other.

WHEN FATE LENDS A HAND

by
BARBARA
COWAN

"A boy! Seven pounds thirteen ounces!" he bellowed up to a smiling couple who were hanging out of the first-floor window above. "Must phone to tell Roger the news. Maggie's fine and so is the baby. Why worry! Nothing else matters!" He threw his arms out expansively as if to embrace the world.

He turned then, and saw me, and with a chuckle he grabbed me and gave me a smacking kiss. Then with a whoop of joy, he turned and took the entrance steps two at a time. I was still smiling when I got into the cab. Only then I noticed the large smudge of cigar ash down the front of my skirt. I did try to brush it away, but on the white material it was still very noticeable.

I bit my lip. This wouldn't help my chances of landing a job. The awful churning in my stomach began, and my interviewing tremble started. Then I thought of the young man — why worry, he'd said. Did I really expect to get the job anyway? Silly to get tied up in knots with nerves. I started smiling again, for the young father's gaiety had infected me.

FIVE minutes later I rang the bell outside the tall terraced house in Glasgow's West End. A worried-looking, middle-aged woman answered it, her hair wispy, as if she hadn't had a chance to tidy it for some time.

"Janet Stewart, I have an appointment at twelve noon." I smiled, looking at my watch, delighted to see there were still two minutes in hand.

"Oh, yes . . . Oh, dear . . . Dr Sanquer has been interviewing since nine this morning . . . He's rather tired . . ."

A roar from a room across the hall interrupted her and she shrugged, then looked at me in a resigned fashion.

"I suppose you'd better go in," she said. "That's him calling."

I gave the worried woman a large smile. Somehow, for the first time at an interview, I wasn't worried about how I looked or what impression I would make. After all, I'd worried about that 24 times already and look where it had got me!

The little woman smiled nervously back and opened the door.

"Come in! Come in!" a male voice roared. "And, Chrissie, I want my lunch at one o'clock."

"Yes, dear, one o'clock. This is — what was the name, Miss . . . ?"

I strode into the room, one hand extended.

"I'm Janet Stewart! And you must be Dr Sanquer. Do you wish me to sit here?" I indicated a leather chair facing his desk.

The middle-aged man glowered and grunted. It sounded like assent, so I sat down, calmly returning his ferocious stare. But he looked away first and I got the impression that under all the bluster he was, like myself, basically shy.

"Type that!" He abruptly shoved a page of barely decipherable writing over the table.

I glanced at it. It was almost as bad as my father's. I remained unruffled.

"One copy or two?" I asked.

I fed the paper into the machine, breathing a sigh of relief. It was an old manual machine, like the one I typed my father's returns on. At some interviews I'd found difficulty with their electric typewriters.

There were a few grammatical and spelling mistakes in the report, so I corrected them as I typed. Then I pulled the paper from the machine, feeling good. Not one mistake!

He took it grudgingly and glanced over it, then over me.

"You've got a dirty mark on your front," he growled.

I flicked lightly at the offending mark and explained briefly, but with some humour, how it happened. Then to my surprise the man guffawed, and seemed to settle back in his chair in a more relaxed manner. Then for about five minutes he fired questions at me.

Soon he knew I had two young brothers and sisters, that my father was a small dairy farmer in Ayrshire with 80 head of cattle, that he and my mother worked the farm themselves, and it *just* supported the family.

Eventually he grunted.

"You're a plain, neat wee thing, but you'll do!" He turned to the little grey-haired woman who was still hovering by the door. "She'll do, won't she? You could live with her around, Chrissie?"

She scuttled over and stood by him.

"Would you mind living in?" she asked anxiously. "You'd have free accommodation — a nice bed-sitter, centrally heated, at the top of the house. My husband . . . Dr Sanquer sometimes works odd hours. Would you mind?"

"Oh, not at all!" I gulped, holding my breath. Was I really being offered a job? "A position with accommodation would be marvellous!" I exclaimed. "Only, my parents would want to see where I was to be living."

"And quite right, too!" Mrs Sanquer suddenly smiled for the first time, the anxious look gone.

The Rainbow

THE rain-storm was heavy, the sky grim and dark,
Yet, very soon after, your delicate arc
Shimmering, glimmering, gloriously bright,
Banded the heavens with ribbons of light.
Orange and primrose, and deep violet-blue,
Apple-green, lilac, how splendid were you!
Our hearts were uplifted, and hope sprang again,
To see your fair promise so soon after rain.
Oh, beautiful rainbow, so briefly you shone,
Just a few precious moments, and then you were gone!

Kathleen O'Farrell.

NOW, I lay and watched the young father as he stood poised at the edge of the pool. Then he dived, his mahogany-coloured body as straight as an arrow, hardly making a splash. An equally brown young woman, carrying a young baby wearing a floppy sun-hat, watched him from the side of the pool. So that was Maggie and the baby, I thought. How I envied their tan.

She quickly handed the baby to a man on a lounger, sitting under the shade of an umbrella. He looked as pale and fair skinned as I had a week ago. Then, she dived into the pool and the two of them swam under water, surfacing to take great gasps of air, sometimes shouting high-spirited insults before they finally clambered out and stood towelling themselves dry.

Then Chrissie bustled out with a tray, bearing drinks for me and Dr Sanquer after our mid-morning swim.

"Come along you two, into the water," she chivvied us. "In you go."
Dr Sanquer pretended to be asleep, but she shook him.
"Hamish, time for your dip!"
He sat up, grumbling.
"Come on, Janet, she'll give us no peace till we go in."
I followed his waddling figure, his rounded stomach overhanging the large swimming shorts. He lowered his considerable bulk into the water, while I washed off my sun-oil under the poolside shower, with Chrissie fussily helping me. Then I climbed down the metal steps into the shallow end of the pool.

"Try not to get your hair too wet, dear," Chrissie cried.

The young parents who were standing nearby exchanged amused glances as I nodded, feeling foolish. I started off, concentrating on my sedate breast stroke, keeping my head well out of the water. As my hand touched the end of the pool, the head of the young father surfaced beside me.

He shook his head vigorously to get the worst of the water out of his hair, and spray flew in all directions.

"My name's Graham Jordan," he announced. "Now it's your turn."
I was a little taken aback.
"Janet Stewart," I murmured.
"Your mother looks after you like a clucking hen." He grinned. "We've been watching."
"My mother wouldn't have time for all that. Aunt Chrissie is a distant relative." I smiled back at his pleasant face, then started back up the pool again. After all, he was someone else's property.

YET, little wonder Chrissie's antics had caught his eye. We'd discovered when my parents came to visit a few days after I started work that her origins were in Ayrshire, too. They went through both family trees and discovered one set of her great-grandparents were my great-great-grandparents on my mother's side. From then on I became family.

At first, as I'd been the eldest of five and never been fussed over, Aunt Chrissie's mothering had been a novelty. Then, gradually, it felt more like smothering and gently I tried to dissuade her. I tried to help her in the house, but she became quite annoyed and immediately re-did

---

The Gift Of Love

DID fate decree this man be mine?
This man I love beyond all time.
Was it planned before our birth?
Or was a search made o'er the earth
To make a match between two souls,
Then let them play predestined rôles?

Whose hand plucked him out for me?
Whose wisdom said this love must be?
Was it God, or just pure chance,
That decided the future of our romance?
But be it fate or be it design,
Thank you for this love of mine.

Barbara Cheshire.

---

anything I'd done, and I felt helpless. I only wanted to do my bit.

"Just thole it, lassie," Dr Sanquer advised me. "We never were blessed with children and she's a born mother. Taken on a new lease of life since you've come, you being kin to her, albeit distant."

WHEN I got to the shallow end and stood up, the young man was at my side again.

"When did you arrive?" he asked me. "We came last night."

"We've been here a week," I murmured, glancing over to his wife who was playing unconcernedly with the baby.

"How long are you staying for?" he asked, unabashed.

"Another two weeks."

Then Aunt Chrissie called, holding up my iced lemonade.

"Janet, once more up and down the pool," she commanded. "And keep your shoulders under water or you'll get burnt."

For once, I was glad of the interruption. I hadn't much experience of young men, but was it quite the thing for a married man to be so persistent? If I was his wife I wouldn't like it.

Obeying Aunt Chrissie, I started down the pool again, but was startled to find Graham Jordan swimming alongside me. I wished I was a strong swimmer, able to reach the end of the pool and immediately turn and swim back. But always when I got there I needed to cling on to regain my breath.

Now, Graham Jordan swimming with me played havoc with my breathing, and I panicked a little, losing my rhythm. Several times I spluttered and gulped in water. Then, when I finally reached out for the edge, it was still just out of my reach, and I almost sank. But Graham Jordan grabbed me as I coughed and spluttered.

"Good thing I was near." He grinned cheerfully. "But you'll be in trouble with your aunt. Your hair is wet!"

Past speaking, my nod was weak. I decided against swimming back to the shallow end and began to heave myself out of the pool to escape. But I faltered halfway out and he happily punted me up the rest of the way.

Still coughing, I staggered back to my lounger, grateful for the cool drink my aunt handed me.

"That young man seemed quite taken with you," she said, eagerly.

"He's married. I think that's his wife and child," I said casually, nodding over to the little group.

"That's never his child." Dr Sanquer grunted. "Belongs to the fellow under the umbrella, I'll be bound. Same red hair."

And, indeed, it was true. The baby's hat was off as the man in the shade now played with him, and their hair colour was identical.

"Those two are probably brother and sister," Dr Sanquer suggested contentedly, balancing his glass of beer on his capacious stomach.

I looked over to where Maggie and Graham were poised again on the edge of the pool. Like a pair of graceful dolphins, they arched into the water. Aunt Chrissie rubbed cream into my back and I sipped my iced lemonade, watching for the two dark heads to rise. Then, when they surfaced, I realised they were calling to one another in fluent Spanish.

And, yes, I could see a resemblance — a strong resemblance. My spirits lifted. And I realised just how often I had relived those few moments when his infectious good humour had changed my outlook.

I supposed that, thanks to him, I'd been more relaxed than usual when I'd arrived for my interview with Dr Sanquer.

I'd worried less about any possible competition I might have for the job and less, too, about what I'd do if I didn't get it.

The Journey

A WINTER'S day,
A church steeple
Half hidden in the mist.
A red-brick farmhouse
Surrounded by naked trees.

A crow circling over a field
Where bright green shoots tease out
Thoughts of spring,
And happy days harvesting . . .

A song thrush perched in a wind-bent
hawthorn,
Its feathers ruffled in the breeze.

A winter's day,
A cream sun half hidden in the mist.

Spring lambs seem far away . . .
Julie Bukowski.

And Graham's exuberant hug and kiss had stayed in my memory, too. Suddenly I really looked forward to the next two weeks. Maybe I'd get to know him better.

But, just then, *she* arrived! Five foot eight of supple grace, smoothly bronzed, and in a miniscule yellow bikini. She hailed the two of them as they clambered out of the water. Miserably, I watched as she joined Graham, supremely sure of herself, not a shy bone in her body.

They both dived back into the water, and she swam strongly, her long hair streaming behind her. My spirits sank to zero as she and Graham surfaced, and she threw her arms around his neck and they disappeared under the surface, kissing. I stumbled to my feet. I didn't want to stay around to watch more. Served me right for being so foolish.

I'LL go and finish typing that report. It's getting a bit too hot now," I murmured, gathering together my bits and pieces before walking to Dr Sanquer's apartment. The Sanquers owned the house in the holiday complex and spent much of the university vacation there. It was delightfully located, overlooking a beautiful bay, bordered by steep, black cliffs.

This three weeks was to be a working holiday for me, for Dr Sanquer could never completely relax, and always had work with him. It was the first time I had been abroad, and it was all so new and wonderful. But now that picture of those two heads disappearing under the water suddenly blotted out all the pleasure I felt about this place. I frowned at myself as I settled down to my typing.

When Fate Lends A Hand

Shortly after, I heard the Sanquers come in, too, which surprised me. We usually stayed by the pool all morning, then had a siesta in the afternoon heat. Had I upset the routine by coming into the apartment early? I had become very fond of them, and they now treated me like a daughter. Yet, sometimes I yearned for young company. Their natural reserve kept them aloof, too, so we seldom met new people, and were constantly in one another's company. I sighed and went on typing.

Then I became aware that Dr Sanquer was laughing, and I could hear Aunt Chrissie's high-pitched voice — and there was another voice, female and young sounding, too. Soon Aunt Chrissie hurried up the small flight of stairs to my room.

"Janet! Janet! We're going to the fiesta tonight! There's to be a band and tables are to be set out around the pool!" she said excitedly. "That was Maggie Patterson," she went on, "the sister of that young man who was speaking to you in the pool.

"Maggie asked very kindly if we would join up with them to fill a table," Aunt Chrissie explained. "She and her husband want to get to know the other residents. It would have seemed churlish to refuse."

My heart leaped at the prospect of the fiesta, but plummeted again at the memory of the Spanish beauty.

Dr Sanquer immediately looked out his cotton trousers and short-sleeved shirt. And Chrissie stood in front of her wardrobe begging me to tell her what would be suitable.

I found myself infected by their excitement, yet it alternated with a feeling of dread. Dr Sanquer had often said I was a neat, plain wee thing, and I dreaded being measured against that gorgeous Spanish girl.

A T half past eight that night when darkness had fallen, and the moon cast a broad path of silver on the bay, the three of us emerged from our apartment. Aunt Chrissie's final choice was a dark skirt, with a frilled blouse, and I'd set her hair. She had used about a kilo of lemons on mine, and it did make a difference.

Unfortunately, I had no trouble choosing what to wear. There was only the dress that I had worn as bridesmaid at my cousin's wedding. It was a cream-coloured muslin with a scooped neckline edged with a frill, as were the sleeves and the hem of the flared, mid-calf skirt. I was rather fond of the dress, but it made me look about 16.

The scene at the poolside was completely changed from this morning. Tables were ranged round it, glasses sparkling in the candlelight, the waiters specially dressed in white shirts and slacks.

We were shown to our table and Maggie Patterson introduced us to her sea-going husband, Roger, then to her brother, Graham, who grinned at me.

"We're on kissing terms already. Remember that day — Roger here was away at sea, and I had all the worry and elation over Maggie and the baby. But it gave me an excuse to kiss the petite little silver-blonde who was waiting for my taxi," he teased.

I found myself blushing, and blessed the darkness for hiding it. So he'd remembered me!

"Oh, here are the twins, Consuela and José!" Maggie exclaimed a moment later.

I looked up to see the tall Spanish girl, now wearing a fashionable black and white culotte outfit, with an equally tall, slim young man. She smiled at me warmly when we were introduced. Then, to my surprise, she sat beside me, and started to give me the story of her childhood in her fractured English.

I soon had the background of Maggie and Graham's Spanish ties. Their aunt was married to Consuela's uncle, and they had spent most summers since their schooldays at their aunt's home in Tenerife. But it puzzled me that Consuela seemed hungrily anxious to hear of my life in Scotland and how I'd spent my childhood.

The Spanish group was playing cheerful music so I was relieved when José asked Consuela to dance. I was free to watch the quick, whole-hearted dancing of the many Spaniards in the company. It wasn't quite like the disco dancing I knew from college!

"Damien, the head waiter, has roped in most of his relatives and their families to swell the numbers," Maggie said, moving into the seat vacated by Consuela. "It's the first time we've had a fiesta here. I'm so glad you've come with your aunt and uncle this year. They never joined in anything before — always just scuttled into their apartment and sat on their terrace. It's important to make this complex a friendly place — and of course I've got an axe to grind — my uncle's the manager . . ."

"Come on, Janet, time you danced with me!" Graham's arm reached out and plucked me from my chair.

"Oh, no, I don't dance like that."

"Time you learned!" He ignored my refusal laughingly.

"Yes, yes, go on, Janet!" Aunt Chrissie beamed, giving me a shove in the direction of the dance floor.

"Now, just keep time to the music and let me lead you," Graham instructed, putting his arm firmly round my waist. But I felt lumpy and awkward, and constantly stumbled over his feet. What must he think? First I couldn't swim and now I couldn't dance.

Then came some kind of set dance, and before I knew it I was pulled into the circle, dragged up and down, under arm, through bridges of arms, crossed over hands, and all at top speed. I almost collapsed when I saw Dr Sanquer and Aunt Chrissie taking part, too. No-one was being allowed to sit out. All reserve was dropped and they joined in the fun. At the end we all limped back, laughing, to our places.

CONSUELA sat for a while, talking earnestly to Dr Sanquer and then got up and grabbed Graham to dance. They made a fine couple, and she never stumbled over his feet or found difficulty with conversation. She seemed to talk non-stop.

But I didn't have time to mull over them as once again I found myself in a circle of Spaniards. This time there was a flamenco flavour to the dance as a youth and a girl danced round one another in the centre. Soon it was my turn and they gave me a good-natured cheer as I threw myself into the spirit of the evening, stamping my feet and twirling.

By this time, I felt so much at ease with everyone that I quite forgot any self-consciousness. All right, I said to myself, even if you can't do this dance authentically, you can at least show you're willing to join in.

"Haven't enjoyed myself so much in years," Dr Sanquer said to me a short time later.

"Me, too!" I agreed. Young men from other tables danced with me, and I was never without a partner. It was wonderful. Once or twice I thought Graham was coming to ask me to partner him, but somehow Consuela always got to him first. So it surprised me when he asked me for the last waltz. I was glad it was a slow dance which I could do.

AND how are you enjoying holidaying here?" he asked, politely. "Does it compare favourably with other places?"

"I don't know. I've never been abroad before," I murmured. "My parents are small farmers, and with five of a family, they could never afford holidays." I lapsed into silence, suddenly shy again.

At this Graham grinned at me.

"Do you know, this morning we decided you were the pampered only child of elderly parents?" When I laughed at that idea, he went on. "Look, there's a fiesta down in the fishing village tomorrow night. Can I take you?

"Mind, there won't be anything fancy or sophisticated. The local people set up tables along the quayside lit by lanterns.

"Then they barbecue all sorts of fish and seafood, and serve it with salad and bread.

"There'll probably be some Spanish dancing, all quite impromptu, but well worth seeing just the same.

"I've been to one or two 'dos' like it in the past and enjoyed myself immensely. Everyone is very friendly. You're really made to feel welcome and to join in the proceedings.

Shafts Of Spring

WE'LL walk together now it's spring,
    And sweet wild pansies peep
    through grass,
And lines of white geese, flying free
    Go squawking, squawking as they
    pass.

We'll linger by a stile to see
    The fleecy lambs play games and run
By new foals munching near the hedge,
    Where green buds open in the sun.

We'll watch a lark against the sky
    Swoop down and down towards the
    stream,
While silver trout swim over stones
    To rest by waterweeds and dream.

We'll stroll through meadows to the hills,
    As sunshine lights the blue above,
Where waking, gold horizons now
    Unfold with promise, like our love.
                    Eileen Sweeney.

105

"In many ways I think that sort of occasion is better than something specially arranged with tourists in mind."

"Won't Consuela mind?" I blurted out, then inwardly raged at myself for being so gauche. Graham would think I was just a country cousin, I told myself.

"Consuela?" he echoed. "She'll come with José. They're to be betrothed on her next birthday."

"José?" I repeated blankly. "But I thought they were twins."

"Oh, no! They're just called that because they're usually inseparable. And have been since they were tots."

"I thought you and she . . ." I floundered, finding difficulty in referring to that kiss between them in the swimming pool, and the way she had monopolised him all evening.

He seemed to sense at once what I was thinking about.

"She's inclined to get over-enthusiastic. I've just persuaded her father to let her come back to Scotland with us for a holiday, and she can talk of little else to me," Graham explained.

"You see, she's never been off the island, and is desperate to know what the rest of the world is like. That's why she collars people like yourself and the Sanquers. She really envies you because you're from Britain. And she'd give anything to have hair and skin the colour of yours, too, and have your calm personality."

"Would she!" I exclaimed, then felt like giggling, thinking of how I had been envying her good looks and poise.

"Will you come to the fiesta, then?" Graham persisted. "I've often thought of you, that little, elfin-like creature I bumped into the day my nephew was born. I feel it's uncanny us meeting again like this."

"I'm flattered you remembered me," I murmured, but was still too shy to admit I'd thought of him, too. "And yes, I'll come."

"Great!" he joked extravagantly. "Now we've got a future to look forward to!"

I smiled. Maybe some day I'd even tell him how his first kiss changed my life! □

DUIRINISH

Duirinish is the most westerly promontory of the island of Skye. Lying close to Dunvegan, the home of the MacLeods, it abounds in clan lore. Two prominent, flat-topped hills are called MacLeod's Tables, while three sea stacks are known as MacLeod's Maidens, referring to a chieftain's wife and daughters who were shipwrecked and drowned there. Also in the Duirinish district is Boreraig, where the MacCrimmons, hereditary pipers to the MacLeods, taught piping for centuries in a cliff hollow used as a piping school. The last MacCrimmon died early in the 19th century, but Boreraig is now the site of a modern Piping Centre.

DUIRINISH, SKYE

IT wasn't often nowadays that Robert Laurence travelled anywhere by train. Usually, on leaving his office in London, he stepped into his big car, driven by Mercer, the chauffeur. In spite of rush-hour traffic, the journey to his home in Surrey was quite fast, as Mercer had long since discovered the best route to take.

On this Thursday evening, however, Mercer and the car were not able to meet him.

There had been a phone call in the afternoon from the worried chauffeur to report that the slight knocking heard in the car during the morning run into town had been the start of something more serious, and some hours' work in a garage

IT'S NEVER TOO LATE

by Christine Maxwell

would be necessary. There was no way the car could be ready for the afternoon journey back into town to meet Mr Laurence.

Tiresome, but not too much of a disaster, thought Robert Laurence, as he reassured Mercer, told his secretary to order a taxi to meet him from the train, and duly set out for Waterloo Station where a train would convey him in half an hour to a small, country station near his home.

So, here he was, settling into a first-class carriage, and noting with disapproval that it hadn't been tidied up since its last journey. Oh well, there probably wasn't time in the rush hour, he conceded, eyeing the discarded newspapers, plastic cups, and other debris present in even a first-class carriage.

Fortunately, on the table in front of him there was nothing but a leaflet someone had left behind. Robert pushed it aside and opened his brief-case, deciding to do a little work on the way home.

Then he paused, his eye caught by the picture on the front of that blue leaflet — a picture of something not often seen now. It was a steam engine puffing its way along a country track. Above were the words: *STRATHSPEY RAILWAY*, and at the bottom of the page he read: *AVIEMORE — BOAT OF GARTEN.*

His attention fully caught now, he opened it out and read what was inside.

Against a background of magnificent scenery, the public can recapture the atmosphere of the Victorian Steam Age, he read.

A small map showed where the train travelled, and a time-table indicated when it ran between the two stations. And as he read, the business world which filled so much of his life these days faded away and he saw himself again as a boy growing up in a small town in Scotland. A hundred yards from his home there was the local railway station, a terminus for the little branch line which came from a junction 10 miles away.

Just as big business absorbed him today, once his thoughts had been constantly on that railway. He'd had the boy's traditional ambition to become an engine driver when he grew up, and by way of preparation he had spent hours at the station, watching and noting all that went on, especially on a Saturday evening when there was a good deal of shunting before the engine was put into a big shed for the weekend.

What was more, he had written a book on the subject! A smile crossed his face now as he recalled the red exercise book where he had recorded the names and numbers of all the engines which came down the line. In his careful, schoolboy handwriting he had described everything he thought interesting, illustrating the book with drawings and photographs. He had been really proud of his effort when he filled in the last page.

Yes, and when he showed it to his friends at the station — the engine-driver and the stoker — they had been full of admiration. Where had that book gone? He hadn't seen it for ages. Had he given it to James? But James wasn't interested in mechanical things . . .

Anyway, it had been a wonderful hobby. Then, suddenly, it seemed that his family were moving. Father was going to succeed an uncle as manager of a big, important firm in London. It was exciting to go there, but naturally there was no longer a quiet, little station for him to keep up his interest in trains.

Robert sighed. He had been sorry to leave that country station. Well, it seemed certain that nowadays there would be no train at all on the line. Even 50 years ago, passengers had been getting fewer as more and more people got cars. And as well as small branch lines, the steam engines had gone, seen now only in museums or at places like the one mentioned in this leaflet someone had left lying on the table.

B UT it was nearly time to leave this train. Robert Laurence put the leaflet in his case and, later on, after the good dinner Mrs Gray, his housekeeper, had set before him, he brought it out and looked at it again.

An irresistible urge came to him to take a weekend off and go north to travel on a steam train once again. It was October now, but the train was still running on Saturdays and Sundays. He looked again and saw this was the last weekend of the season. Then he lifted his telephone.

In 10 minutes everything was settled. He would travel north tomorrow, stay at a hotel in Aviemore, and go on the steam train next day. He wouldn't tell anyone, though, why he was going there. Mercer and Mrs Gray would stare and wonder at the master doing such a strange thing. No, they wouldn't understand, so he would just let them think he was going on one of his frequent business trips.

For a moment his eye rested on the photograph of a young woman which stood on his desk. She would have understood. Oh, it was a lonely thing getting through life without the wife he had loved so deeply for five years. Why had she to die so young? It had been a shattering blow, and he still missed her, with her bright ways and warm love for him.

He hadn't been quite alone, of course, when Catherine died. There had been his four-year-old son, bewildered and unhappy, turning to his busy father for comfort in a way which brought them very close for a time.

But the child had grown up and now he, too, was gone, killed in an accident on the Swiss mountains. Now Robert dwelt for a moment on his own anger when James had told him bravely that his heart wasn't in the world of business, but out in the keen, cold air of the mountains.

"I would really like to train as a ski instructor," the young man had said eagerly. "They need lots of people for that and I'm sure I could get a job in time. It's such a marvellous country and I . . . I've made friends."

Robert had soon discovered the real reason why James yearned for an outdoor life on the hills. It was a girl he had met there, actually a Scottish girl who worked in one of the hotels and knew all there was to know about skiing.

"We love each other, Dad," James had said earnestly. "We think the same way, like the same things, and we plan to be married quite soon. She hasn't any folk of her own, you see, she doesn't even remember her parents."

"Married?" Robert had been astounded. "Are you mad, boy? You're what — twenty? It's out of the question!"

BUT James had gone off after the disastrous quarrel, and he had married Sue Elder. A year later, a letter had come for him announcing the birth of a son.

So You Think You Know About Scotland?

1. In which town did the King sit "drinking blude-red wine"?
2. What is the meaning of King Malcolm Canmore's surname?
3. How many Maries did Mary Queen of Scots have?
4. Who said of the Stewart throne, "It cam' wi' a lass and it will gang wi' a lass"?
5. Who is the present-day Lord Of The Isles?

Answers below.

1. Dunfermline.
2. Big head.
3. Four.
4. James V.
5. Prince Charles.

"His name's to be Craig," James wrote. "We hope to be living in Britain again before long, up in the Scottish Highlands, so perhaps you would like to see your grandson."

Robert hadn't answered the letter. Often he wished he had done so, because only weeks later news had come of the accident and the death of his son. So the money he had lavished on the boy and the first-class education he had given him — all went for nothing, he thought bitterly. The dream of seeing James as yet another Laurence who was chairman of the big London firm would never now be more than a dream.

However, he had done the right thing by the girl his son had married, arranging that each month a handsome cheque was paid into her bank account. He had half expected the girl to refuse this help in a foolishly proud manner, but that hadn't happened. What she did with the money he had no idea, but at least it meant the boy could be properly educated.

How old would he be now? About eight years old, Robert supposed, as he put his hand on the bell to summon Mrs Gray. He must let her know he would be away for the weekend.

Mrs Gray was well used to his travelling about all over the place. She waited while he wrote the name and address of the hotel where he would be staying, just in case any crisis arose requiring his presence.

Child's Eye

MY morals you don't question,
    My reasons — you don't pry.
You see me so simplistically
    With yours, the child's eye.

My money you don't count.
    My clothes you do not mock.
You give and take love freely,
    My touch gives you no shock.

My smile to you is just a smile.
    My tears you wipe away.
Emotions are emotions,
    Not a game for you to play.

My politics don't matter.
    My colour — you don't care.
You get the greatest pleasure,
    In me just being there.

How my vision's tarnished.
    How I wish that it were I,
To see things with such beauty,
    Through yours, the child's eye.

                    M Sanders.

GLANCING at the bit of paper as she took it, she gave a start.
    "Oh, Mr Laurence!" she exclaimed. "You're going to Aviemore! Are you — you will be going to see Mrs James? I mean . . ."
She broke off as he frowned at her.
    "I'm not going to see anyone," he retorted. "What do you mean, Mrs James?"
The housekeeper looked back at him.
    "Surely you know your son's wife lives at Aviemore," she said quietly. "I'm sorry, sir, I just thought perhaps you were going up to see her and — and the little boy."
    "No, it's something quite different," he muttered.
    Left alone, he almost phoned to cancel the arrangements he had made. But, no, he could still go and fulfil this urge to travel on the steam train. Aviemore must be a big enough place to stay in for a short weekend without encountering his daughter-in-law.

It's Never Too Late

Strange how he hadn't realised that was where she was staying. Now he began to recollect a formal letter from the bank informing him that Mrs Susan Laurence had moved to Scotland. Had he still got that letter? It had come years ago.

A search through his orderly desk discovered the letter containing the address. It conveyed nothing to him, he still didn't know whether it was near the centre of the town or not.

Well, he wouldn't be calling at that address, but he was still going to Scotland. There must be other steam railways nearer, but he had made up his mind to go on that one.

THE long journey north next day proved rather enjoyable. Robert got through quite a lot of paper work, and was ready to relax when he finally left the train soon after seven o'clock. The hotel where a booking had been made for him was just across the road from the station, and after a good meal he felt a pleasant sense of anticipation about what was to happen next day.

In the morning he took a stroll round the place. Occasionally he saw a boy who might be about eight years old, and wondered vaguely if it could be his grandson. He thought he would have recognised the boy's mother, though he had only seen her once, at the funeral service for James which he had insisted on arranging. His recollection was of a pale girl trying vainly to stop the tears which rolled down her face.

At last it was time to go for the steam train. He set off for the station, a little apart from the main line one, and the thought came to him that if this had been a film, then he would find himself seated in a carriage beside his daughter-in-law and grandson!

Fortunately, coincidences like that didn't often happen in real life. The only other passengers in his compartment were a man about his own age, and a little boy probably about six or seven.

The man was a chatty type, not in the least discouraged by the brief answers he got from Robert. He described how every now and then he took the boy on this journey, and they were coming today because it was the last chance this year.

"But we'll be able to come again next year, won't we, Grandad?" asked the boy anxiously.

"Yes, Harry, they'll be starting up again at Easter time."

"Can we come the very first day, Grandad?"

"Oh, I expect so!"

The man smiled affectionately at young Harry, then looked across at Robert.

"That boy keeps me young!" he announced. "Anyway, I know now why grandfathers are called that. It's because it's grand to be one!"

Robert said nothing. He studied his map and looked out at the scenery through which they were passing, some of the trees already turning to vibrant red and gold.

It was good to hear the old familiar sound of a steam engine as it puffed its way along. He liked hearing the whistle, too. These big, modern engines didn't make the same sound at all.

Boat of Garten Station took him right back into the past for it looked like the country station he remembered near his childhood home. He could see many things from a former age, and it was the same when he went inside a small museum where there was an interesting collection of old timetables, photographs and tools once used.

Outside again, he crossed the high bridge to look at carriages which stood in a siding. There was so much of interest to see here.

It was in the well-stocked railway shop that he encountered his fellow-passenger and the little boy. Harry was begging for one of the caps offered for sale with *STRATHSPEY RAILWAY* on the front of it.

"Harry, you've got one at home," the grandfather protested.

"I don't know where it is," the boy lamented. "I want to put one on now, then when we get back to Aviemore and walk home everyone will know where I've been. Oh, please, Grandad!"

The caps cost 50p and Robert was never sure why the impulse came to him to buy one. He handed it to Harry and saw the boy's eyes sparkle.

"Oh, thank you! Thanks a million!" he exclaimed. Then in an earnest tone he confided: "You see, I'm going to be an engine driver when I grow up." "They all say that." His grandfather beamed.

A S they left the shop Robert looked after them. What good friends they seemed, just as he had been once, for a time, with his son James. Then he had become so busy, so absorbed in the world of business, that the closeness seemed to fade. And now he had no son,

---

Memories

I SIT alone and wonder,
  Why it should be so,
That I hear so clearly voices,
  From the distant, long ago.

Little laddies shouting,
  Who must be retired men.
Little lassies laughing,
  Who'll ne'er see sixty-one again.

I hear the songs of fisherlads,
  Setting out to sea.
Melodies that dance bands played,
  When I was twenty-three.

Hymns the choir practised,
  In the long-gone, village hall.
Songs we sang, when playing ball,
  Against the schoolhouse wall.

I hear the village worthies,
  Long sleeping, in the grave,
Talking of "the good old days."
  Recall the good advice they gave.

Maybe it's my mind that's gone,
  Now that I'm ninety-three.
I'd best rise up, and stir myself,
  And make a good, strong, cup of tea.

Macdonald Palmer.

just a grandson he had never seen. What was it that man had said? *It's just grand being a grandfather.*

I am one, Robert thought. I could go back to Aviemore and see my grandson. He'll be a little older than that boy. I wonder if he's been on this steam railway.

Living in Aviemore, it seemed likely. Was he interested in trains? Did he, too, want to be an engine driver some day?

I don't know, Robert thought. I don't know a thing about him, except that they called him Craig.

Was that because the name reminded his parents of the mountains and rocks they both loved? As he sat in the quiet station, waiting for the train to come back from another journey to Aviemore, Robert felt he was in a different world from the one he knew best. It seemed a gentler, kindlier world than the one he had built around himself for so long. But in any sort of world it was surely never too late to make right what had been wrong.

H IS resolve grew. Once back at Aviemore, he asked the way to that address his mind had retained. It took only five minutes to get there, and he paused for a moment as he looked at the small, neat cottage with a garden in front.

Strathspey Railway Facts

The Strathspey Railway opened for business in the summer of 1978.

The line runs for five miles between Aviemore and Boat of Garten.

The livery of the rolling stock is off-white on the upper half and purple lake (a dark brown/purple colour) below.

The Strathspey Railway has its own newsletter, the Strathspey Express.

Would he be welcome there? Or would the door be shut in his face? It would be no more than he deserved.

At last, he went up the short path and rang the bell.

The door was opened by Sue Laurence. She looked back inquiringly, then suddenly flushed as she recovnised who stood there.

"It . . . it's Mr Laurence?" she stammered.

"Yes, I came to —"

Robert stopped short, for once at a loss for words. Then the awkward moment passed as Sue Laurence spoke quietly.

"Please come in."

Robert followed her inside and into a living-room where an eight-year-old boy knelt on the floor, constructing some sort of model. Dark hair and dark eyes — it came as a shock to Robert to see how like James he was. It could have been his son there, glancing up to see who had come in.

"It's your grandfather, Craig," his mother said.

CRAIG got to his feet, looking back uncertainly while Robert was glad to sink into an easy chair. What did a man say to the grandson he had ignored for all those years, a grandson who was the image of the son he had loved?

Strathspey Railway Facts

The first locomotive for the Strathspey Railway was presented by the Scottish Gas Board.

One of the locomotives on the line was rescued from a scrap-yard.

The turntable at Speyside Station, Aviemore, was also rescued — from Kyle of Lochalsh.

All the railway staff are voluntary and unpaid.

"I was just making a cup of tea," Sue said. "The kettle will be boiling."

She left the room. Robert had never felt so awkward in his life, so unsure of what to say or do next. At last he managed to get out a few words.

"What's that you are making?" he inquired.

"A railway engine," the boy answered. "A steam one, like they have on the Strathspey line here."

"I've just been on that line," Robert told him gravely. "I expect you have a journey sometimes?"

Craig nodded. Then suddenly he turned and ran from the room. Robert's heart sank. But he couldn't blame the boy . . .

Craig was back, pulling something out of the big envelope he carried. It was a red exercise book.

"Are you my grandfather who wrote this book?" he asked. "My mummy says you did it when you were a little boy. I think it's awfully good."

So James did have the book! And when he died Sue hadn't thrown it out, but kept it for Craig when he grew old enough to appreciate it. The interest in railways was what she had described to the child when she might well have told him his grandfather was unkind and unfriendly.

It was deep remorse Robert felt now, and a bitter regret for those wasted years when he could have done so much more than merely send money which he had never missed. Oh, he must make up for it somehow!

With an effort he pulled himself together and answered Craig's questions about some of the drawings in the book. Yes, that big lever was what you moved to make the engine go. And that strange-looking engine he had drawn one weekend was a very old one, called back temporarily into service.

SUE carried a tray into the room.
"Craig loves that book," she said with a smile. "He's so interested in railways and his idea of bliss is to travel on the steam train —"
"Tomorrow's the last day for this year," Craig broke in. "Can you really not take me, Mummy?" he asked anxiously.

Sue shook her head, turning to explain to Robert. She had agreed to take charge of her neighbours' two small children for the afternoon while their parents went to visit someone in an Inverness hospital.

"Eight-month-old twins aren't quite the age to go on the train." She sighed. "Not these two anyway!"

Robert looked back at her.

"Would you allow me to take Craig on the train tomorrow?" he suggested. "I was on it today and would really like to go again."

Sue gave her permission and Craig was jubilant.

Keep Smiling

LET'S all make a little vow,
 Starting from today,
To find the very best in life,
 Whate'er may come our way.
Learning to be patient,
 When we're oft inclined to snap,
Keeping cool and calm,
 Instead of whirling in a flap!
Showing off a chirpy smile
 To banish that old frown,
Making sure we really won't
 Let upsets get us down.
Kindliness spreads far and wide,
 Brings happiness each day.
The cost is small, the value great.
 The thought in hearts will stay.

Elizabeth Gozney.

So tomorrow, thought Robert, he would make the journey again, along with his grandson, just like that man he had met this afternoon. But still the thought of these wasted years nagged at him, and when, later on, Sue spoke of that money he hardly knew where to look.

"Your kind gifts have helped Craig and me so much," she told him in her quiet way. "It means I can manage with just part-time work, so I can always be here when he isn't at school. And we thought you would come to see us one day when you weren't too busy. We were right about that."

"While I was wrong about everything," murmured Robert. "I know now why James loved you and married you, Sue.

"Will you bring Craig to see me sometimes, or is that too much to ask? I want to find out if it really is true what someone told me, that being a grandfather is just grand."

Sue gave back a warm, forgiving smile.

"But of course it is," she said. □

The Meaning

f Christmas

by Laura Caldwell

THE telephone call from Edinburgh reached Jon Mayrin at eight o'clock in the morning. Twenty minutes later he was in a taxi heading for Geneva's airport. He knew a plane for Heathrow took off at nine o'clock, and he prayed a stand-by seat would be available. There had been no time to book. No time for anything, except that he must get himself to Scotland quickly, quickly.

He was lucky. The plane took off into the pale, wintry sky above Switzerland and Jon was on it. When he arrived at Heathrow, he would take a plane north, and a fast cab to Edinburgh's Royal Infirmary.

As the plane zoomed higher and higher till the mountain peaks looked like sugar-loaf hats, and the lakes resembled pudding-basin pools, Jon Mayrin, teacher of English at a Geneva college, closed his eyes. He recalled the traumatic message which had precipitated his departure.

"Jon, I have such terrible news." It was the voice of his father-in-law. "Morag has been seriously hurt in an accident. The taxi she was travelling in from Turnhouse to our home skidded and hit a wall. She is in Intensive Care . . ." He had spoken for just another minute, his message leaving Jon in a state of shock.

Now the young Swiss tried to calm his nightmare thoughts. How stupid, how blindly stupid he had been!

"But, Jon, you promised." He heard again Morag's voice. And his own cold reply: "Not so. All I said was I'd *probably* be with you."

"Oh, why do you have to quibble over words?" she'd said. "I believed all along you would be coming."

"My dear, I cannot let my students down. They've been working so hard on this play," he had told her.

"I know — but . . ."

He had interrupted her. "And now you also know that the performances are fixed for Christmas Eve, Christmas Day, and New Year's Day."

His wife had protested then — "I never thought this would happen."

"And neither did I!" Jon had exclaimed. "I understood we were to perform on Twelfth Night only. It was not my doing that the programme dates were altered at the last minute."

Morag's voice was ominously low when she had answered him.

"So you have made up your mind then? You consider your students more important than me?"

"Now you are being absurd. We will have Christmas together, my love. The play will take up just a few hours in the late evenings. Try to

119

understand." Jon's features had taken on that closed, locked-in look Morag was beginning to know so well.

"All right, Jon, you celebrate this Christmas with your students. I will go home to Edinburgh on my own."

But her husband's blue eyes had blazed with anger.

"No! I want you here by my side. You must meet my students. You will stay here in Geneva over Christmas." His wife was silent. "Do you hear me, Morag?"

"Yes, I hear you. Nevertheless I've no intention of disappointing my parents. I shall go to Edinburgh without you."

Jon Mayrin was Swiss born, but his native tongue was German, and there was a measure of German aggression in his make-up. He had assumed all along Morag would give in, remain — as was her place — with him. He was dismayed.

"Listen, my darling," he tried another approach. "We will have such a happy time here. We will celebrate with parties and entertainment. Perhaps some skiing, some sleigh-rides? You do not forget the Escalade Festival when we rode on the pony-sleigh around the villages, and all the bells rang out for us?"

MORAG MAYRIN had closed her eyes then. How could she forget the Christmas of the sleigh-rides? Never, never. Her love for Jon and his for her had been at its peak then, exactly one year ago. Wrapped in furs, her young husband's strong arm about her, they had been transported through the frosty moonlit night as if in a fairy coach, with tinkling bell-music all the way. The Festival, the ancient Swiss festival of young lovers visiting friends and relations in outlying farms and villages by pony-sleigh, would stay in her memory for ever.

Remembering this happy time she had almost relented, but she steeled herself.

"Jon, darling, try to understand. My parents are elderly, I am their only daughter and I promised I would be with them this Christmas."

"They are not to be alone. Your brother Gavin is to be there."

"That's another reason I want so much to be in Edinburgh. I haven't seen Gavin since our wedding." Morag's brother lived and worked in Canada. In the summer he had married a Toronto girl and was bringing her home to meet his family this Christmas.

"But Gavin and his wife can come here to us at any time, I would welcome them for a holiday." Jon was losing patience.

It was useless. There was no getting through to Jon once he had made up his mind. After 2½ years of marriage to the handsome young Swiss, Morag was becoming more and more aware of this. But she determined she, too, would not give in and quietly she made her own plans for Christmas.

Her mind was troubled, though. What was happening to their marriage? They had been so much in love, she and Jon. Longing to be together always. And now? It was as if somewhere along the line they had lost communication with each other. And Morag blamed her husband.

This latest demonstration — forbidding her to go to her parents' home without him — she thought of sadly as a clear signpost to what she called his selfish chauvinistic attitude.

Lying by the side of her sleeping husband on the night before she left for Scotland, Morag Mayrin couldn't sleep. Her wide-awake mind turned over and over, recalling unhappy little incidents. Of course, she had known when she married Jon how dedicated he was to having a successful career. Where his pupils were concerned nothing was too great a trouble.

"One day I mean to become a professor," he was fond of saying. "The way is clear, it is in my own hands. I think often, Morag, about my father and how he would tell me, 'Give of your best always, my son, and the best will come back to you.' "

When he had first recounted the solemn words to her, Morag had burst out laughing.

"Oh, Jon, you can be so — so *pompous*, sometimes!"

"*Pom-pus?* What is pom-pus?"

"Well, conceited — no, not that really, just sort of humourless, taking everything with such deadly seriousness." And, still laughing, she had put her arms about his neck and gently tickled him till he was forced to laugh.

"That's it, my darling, solemn schoolmaster." She'd giggled. "You must smile more, laugh more."

Jon had seized his teasing wife then, clasped her in a bear-hug, forced her head back and kissed her throat, her cheeks, her lovely inviting mouth till she cried out.

"Jon! Please — don't be so fierce! Your kisses hurt . . ."

"So, I am fierce also, am I? And a pom-pus bore as well, yes?"

"No, no, not a bore, never that! I'll try to explain . . ." But Morag hadn't bothered to explain, instead she snuggled close. Jon's kisses maybe sometimes hurt, but they also unfailingly spun her dizzily into another world, that fantastic world of joyous lovemaking they shared.

THE Swiss plane dipped low over London, over the snaking dark line of the Thames, the gleaming buildings, the patches of green.

It was here in London, three years ago, Jon Mayrin had first met Morag Hay. He was attending a school of languages to perfect his English, and Morag was working as a typist in a Government office. She shared a flat with two other girls, and Jon occupied a room on the floor above. He used to wait till he heard her door slam shut in the morning, then hurtle downstairs.

"Ah, good morning!" He would bow from the waist, apparently totally surprised at their meeting! Right from the first moment he set eyes on her, Jon had found Morag irresistibly attractive. Her voice was different — he guessed this must be a Scottish accent; her hair shone like bronze, and she had beautiful, laughing, hazel eyes and inviting lips. He lost no time in asking her out.

"This new film in town, perhaps you would come with me to see it?" And that was how it all began.

The People's Friend Annual

Morag, too, was a newcomer to London. She was hard-up and had to budget carefully. But together they explored the city, window-shopped, sailed down the river. Jon had an allowance from his father.

"My father is anxious only that I do well, reach the top," he had explained. Perhaps she should have been warned by this too-dedicated determination to "get on!" But for them both it was a genuine case of love at first sight. These first few months in London had been a halcyon time.

A HOUSEWIFE'S ARMOUR

IN olden days, they say, knights kept vigil in some lonesome forest chapel on the eve of their departing on a saintly quest.

Thus all around the altar, in the cold moonlight, lay the knight's sword and helmet, his lance and breast-plate in dedication.

A romantic ideal, born of the vision and dreams of poets.

Why discount romance and its magic touch on life?

I think of the housewife and her routine drudgery of daily, humdrum tasks. I think of her apron — protection from the kitchen's lowliest tasks, of her overall for household chores.

They are the humblest of garments. Yet are they not her armour? Worn in the worthy service her household expects of her? She fills the role of a knight of old!

Rev. T. R. S. Campbell.

AS soon as he reached Heathrow, Jon hurried to find a kiosk, and called the Hay home, but there was no answer. This total lack of contact had a worsening effect on his state of mind. He could think of nothing — nothing but his young wife and what he might soon have to face. It was a relief to get on the north-bound plane.

This was Jon's third visit to Edinburgh, and Morag's home. His first had been when they became engaged.

"Of course Mum and Dad are eager to meet you, Jon," she'd told him. "And I want to show you off!"

"I feel nervous, darling," he had replied quite seriously.

"And, goodness me, so you should be! My father has this dreadful habit of chasing all my boyfriends away. He's as stern and prickly as a six-foot thistle. So watch out, love."

"Stop teasing!" Jon had admonished her. "To meet one's future father and mother-in-law is a very serious matter, Morag. Are you never serious about anything?"

"Oh, sometimes . . . When I'm in the mood."

"Shall I put you in the mood?" No matter how solemn Jon could sometimes be, his love-making — Morag found — set all the world to rights again.

And Jon had found Bert and Dorothy Hay warm-hearted and

welcoming, eager to make this visitor from abroad feel at home.

His next visit to Edinburgh had been for his own wedding on a golden day in June. All the bells in the land seemed to be ringing out for the handsome Swiss schoolmaster and his radiant Scottish bride.

In their first year of marriage Jon had taught English in a senior Geneva school. Morag knew she had married a brilliant young man, and so she was not at all surprised when he was offered an appointment as a college lecturer. But it was in the months following this she began to notice changes in her husband.

She had found work in a Swiss tourist office and each morning the young husband and wife left their neat flat in Rue Kloster together. Morag was always first to return, which gave her time to prepare their evening meal. But as the winter wore on Jon was coming home later and later.

At first he was full of apologies.

"I am sorry, darling, there was this student who wanted to discuss his work with me." Or, "Sorry, Morag, but I had so many notes to write up." Then on a night when he was very late — "I called an extra meeting for this evening, I meant to tell you. My students are putting on a play for Twelfth Night and I have to produce it. It will mean many rehearsals, much hard work."

Morag began to feel left out and unhappy. There had been a time when Jon was more than content to spend his evenings with her — not that they had been idle evenings.

As a child his father had taught him the art of wood-carving, and this was now his greatest hobby. He had made a jewel-box for her, and a tiny robin perched on a twig.

And after those fantastic sleigh-rides last Christmas he carved a small sleigh and high-stepping pony with flying mane. He fixed little bells to the scarlet leather reins, and concealed a musical box within the passengers' seat.

When he presented it to Morag on their first wedding anniversary, he pressed the switch and the tiny tinkling melody rang out —

Jingle bells, jingle bells,
Jingle all the way.
Oh what fun it is to ride
In a one-horse open sleigh.

Morag was enchanted with the lovely gift and, although it was June and high summer, she played it and played it until Jon had cried for mercy.

"Please, please, my love, hide it away until Christmas! We cannot go sleigh-riding while the city wilts in a heatwave!" They had laughed then, and obediently she had tucked the little sleigh away.

AT once, please, the Royal Infirmary." Jon Mayrin's voice as he hailed a taxi at Turnhouse Airport was vibrant with urgency.

At the hospital he was directed to a small waiting-room. He was not surprised to find Morag's parents there. He greeted them and then waited, afraid to put the first question.

"There is no change," Bert Hay told him without being asked. "She is deeply unconscious. We've been told to wait here until the doctor comes."

There was a silence before Morag's mother spoke, obviously distressed but in control of herself.

"We didn't know Morag was coming to us alone, Jon. We thought you were both to be with us over Christmas."

Dorothy Hay's gently-spoken words seemed instantly to expose her son-in-law's guilt.

"I — wasn't able to get away. My students . . ." Jon stopped and put a hand up to cover his eyes. *His students!* Well, what was happening now to his students? They would perform the play he had directed with such care and given so much, so very much precious time to. Of course the show would go on.

Why had he ever thought he was indispensable? How had he got his priorities so badly wrong? Did it really matter above all else that one day he should be offered a professorship? For that had been the motive behind his working, working, early and late — and neglecting his lovely Morag.

He heard again his father's solemn voice — "Give of your best always, my son, and the best will come back to you." What had his father meant? Best in the fight to "get on," of course! What about the human factor? What about loving relationships? Had he given his best to Morag? Had he?

The door of the waiting-room opened.

"Mr Mayrin, you can see your wife now." The doctor walked the length of the long corridor, Jon by his side. "Your wife is in a coma, deeply unconscious. The next few days will tell us one way or the other."

The nurse who was seated at Morag's bedside went out as the doctor showed Jon in, then left him alone with his wife.

The young husband felt suddenly weak. This could not be Morag, his beautiful laughing Morag, propped on pillows, her eyes closed, her face white and empty. And those tubes, the glass vessels, all the clinical machinery of Intensive Care . . .

He sat close to her murmuring words of endearment.

"Morag — Morag, my darling . . ." The closed eyes did not move. "This is Jon, my love. I've come — I've come to be beside you . . ." He talked on, willing her to move, to respond. But there was nothing — nothing. Jon Mayrin bowed his head and wept.

IT was a sad little party who sat round the supper table that night in Bert and Dorothy's house. Morag's brother Gavin, and Liz, his wife, had arrived from Canada two days before, and were stunned at what had happened.

Later, Jon slept fitfully, his shocked senses spelling out the possible truth that had he been with Morag on the trip to Scotland, the pattern would have been different, the terrible accident never happened.

Next morning at her bedside the doctor had some advice for Jon.

"Talk to your wife, Mr Mayrin, keep on talking," he said. "Recall happy times — sing, laugh aloud if you can. It is of vital importance you try to reach her. Keep on trying."

And so Jon sat alone and talked and talked, stopping only when he felt too drained emotionally to go on.

Leaving the hospital he did not return at once to the Hays' home. Instead his footsteps led him, like someone in a dream, down the Mound and on to Princes Street. Edinburgh, like his own Geneva, was bright for Christmas, the pavements and the shops crowded. In his dark hour of sadness it was all too much for the young husband. He turned and began a slow walk back up the Mound.

The giant Christmas tree, an annual gift from Norway, glittered with lights in its place on the green slopes. And pricked out in red and silver lights on the grass, alongside the tree, there was the outline of a sleigh and prancing reindeer.

The brilliant Christmas spectacle brought Jon to a sudden halt. He stared as if bewitched, clasping the iron railing till his knuckles shone white, his heart racing.

The pretty scene, so familiar yet so fresh with each successive Christmas, triggered off the beginnings of an idea for him.

DEEP in thought, Jon slowly retraced his footsteps towards Princes Street. Could he do it, he wondered? Even more important, would his idea work?

He had nothing to lose, he decided, and so very much to win.

Now that his mind was made up, Jon strode out briskly. He had arrangements to make, timings to check.

Suddenly he saw the old, grey city, which had earlier seemed to live up to its reputation of being withdrawn and cold, through new eyes.

So You Think You Know About Scotland?

1. At which castle was the Marquis of Montrose held prisoner in 1650 before being handed over to the government forces?
2. In which castle is Scotland's National War Museum?
3. Which Angus castle was burned down by the Duke of Argyll in 1640 and is commemorated in a ballad?

Answers below.

1. Ardvreck, Sutherland.
2. Edinburgh.
3. The Bonnie Hoose O' Airlie.

His wife loved this ancient capital, he told himself, and he would learn to love it, too — its Georgian squares in the New Town, the old buildings crowding towards each other on the long ridge from the Castle to Holyrood House.

After the hectic couple of hours, Jon went into a coffee shop and ordered a coffee and a piece of shortbread. As he sat, welcoming the warm fug after the frosty weather outside, he ran through a mental check-list. Yes, he'd attended to everything.

Morag's parents were dismayed when their son-in-law made his announcement at midday.

"I have to return to Geneva today, at once." His words were met with looks of bewilderment. "Please — accept that I must go. I will be back tomorrow. Then I promise you I will tell you what this is all about."

Jon flew to Heathrow on the three o'clock plane. Before eight o'clock that evening he was opening the door of his flat with shaking hands.

The sight of all the old familiar things — his wife's knitting, a half-completed sweater for himself, her library novel, the scent of summer flowers, of Morag, when he flung open her wardrobe door, caught at his very heart-strings.

He took a sheepskin muff from a shelf, and felt around for another small object. He found what he was looking for and placed it carefully inside the muff.

His mission accomplished, Jon was on the early plane for London next morning. The sheepskin muff and its contents were safe in his overnight bag which never left his side.

H E went straight to the hospital, and he was allowed to see his wife at once.

"I'm sorry, there's no change," the doctor told him then left him alone.

Jon sat by Morag's bed and began at once to talk.

"I've been back home, my darling," he said tenderly. "The flat is looking so welcoming, so homely. The sweater you are knitting for me is waiting ready for you to pick it up, and the new novel from the library you were so eager to read is waiting for you also." Now he drew the sheepskin muff from his bag. "I've brought this, Morag. Remember the pretty muff you always took on our sleigh-rides? Touch it, my love, feel it . . ." Jon stroked the small motionless hands with the soft fleece.

It seemed to him — and he thought his heart would stop — as if her fingers momentarily quivered. But then all was stillness again. Had he imagined the brief movement? Had it been simply the result of wishful thinking? He went on talking, recalling last Christmas.

"Do you remember the music of the bells, and the snow-spray flying up from the pony's hooves?" He drew from the muff the little toy he had sheltered in its protecting depths. It was his gift to Morag on their first wedding anniversary, the high-stepping pony and sleigh carved so beautifully out of wood and fitted with tiny bells and a musical box.

"Listen, listen, my love, do you remember?" Jon touched the switch and the fairy-like music tinkled out —

Jingle bells, jingle bells,
Jingle all the way,
Oh what fun it is to ride
In a one-horse open sleigh

The Meaning Of Christmas

He played it over and over again. He shook the prancing pony so that the sad hospital room was filled with the sound of silvery bells. He held it close, close to his beloved young wife.

"Listen! Listen! My love, you must hear it . . . you must." But the white mask of Morag's face on the pillow did not change expression.

The doctor came back and a nurse followed. Jon's time was up.

"Mr Mayrin!" Jon was halfway down the long corridor when the nurse caught up with him. "The doctor wants you to come back."

Fearful for what might be before him he turned and the doctor motioned Jon to Morag's side.

"Take her hands in yours, please," he said quietly.

The hands Jon held quivered, he felt a warmth begin to flow, and only then did he look directly at the face on the pillow. *Morag's eyes were open.* This was the turning-point — an urgent, vibrant, life-giving force was taking over!

"You had just left the room when we saw her eyes flicker and slowly open." The doctor's voice thrilled with excitement, his dark eyes held all the happiness which is the reward of caring doctors the world over. It was the triumph of life over death.

"Have you been talking to your wife about something which might have . . . ?" he asked Jon.

"I talked about last Christmas, about sleigh-rides in the snow. I let her hear the jingle of the bells. And I talked about love — just love."

The good doctor smiled.

"What else is Christmas all about?" he said.

CHRISTMAS went by, the new year began. Spring came to Switzerland with brilliant patchworks of wild flowers on the mountain slopes, and fierce waterfalls of melting snow. And Morag Mayrin returned at last to her home in Geneva.

Recovery had been slow but sure and now her heart was filled with thankfulness as Jon, a smiling Jon, excited as a little boy, took her on a tour of their flat.

"See," he exclaimed proudly. "I have painted the sitting-room! What do you think of my work, eh? If I am thrown out of my college for refusing from now on to work overtime, do you think I could find employment as a painter?" he teased. "As a handyman?"

Morag, admiring everything, assured him she had a very talented young husband!

"And there is something else, my darling," Jon murmured tenderly. "Something which is very important to us both!"

Her gaze went slowly round the room, and then she saw it! Standing on the broad windowsill was the little sleigh and prancing pony, its scarlet leather harness and tiny bells twinkling. Propped against one small hoof was a card and she picked it up.

Please do not hide me away, she read. *Spring, summer, autumn, winter — take time always to listen to the joyful bells of love.*

Morag Mayrin could not speak. But Jon acted quickly. He took her in his arms and kissed — and kissed — her. □

Where The

Heart Lies

by
JEAN MELVILLE

HEATHER MUNRO swallowed a lump in her throat as the removal men began to lift out the largest pieces of furniture from Aunt Hannah's drawing-room. It was sad to see the break-up of the old house which she had loved so much as a child. In fact, it had been her home from the age of five when her parents died, until she was nineteen.

Aunt Hannah, her father's sister, had never married, but she had meant everything to the small, bewildered girl who had suddenly exchanged life in a busy London flat for life in a small Scottish village. She was the postmistress at Locharin, and one of the two larger rooms at the front of the house had been converted into the village post office.

Everyone in Locharin knew and loved Miss Munro, but two years ago the post office had been closed and the villagers were obliged to go to Brechinbridge, three miles away on the Edinburgh road. Hannah Munro had retired and quietly closed the door on the room which had been so much part of her life. How lonely she must have been, Heather thought sadly, as she packed a box of bric-a-brac for charity.

A little over two years ago she had left the old house to go back to London. She had often wondered how much Aunt Hannah had guessed about her real reason for wanting to go.

"Come back as often as you can, Heather," she'd said, looking at her with uncertain eyes.

"Every holiday, Auntie darling," she'd promised.

But, in London, she had met Simon Watson and he had claimed most of her attention. She had not come home to Locharin as often as she should, but Aunt Hannah seemed to understand.

Johnnie McBride was still living next door, and Heather was not yet ready to face him again. She had loved him since she was a child, and thought that he loved her.

It had been hard to face the fact that Johnnie's love for her was what he might have felt for a younger sister. Her own love had matured from that of a child into that of a woman, but Johnnie's had remained the same warm affection and kindness he had always felt.

He had allowed her to boss him about as a child, and had readily done her bidding. As they grew up, it was Johnnie who accompanied her everywhere, to dances and parties, partnering her at tennis and badminton.

Heather had taken him for granted and her cheeks often burned with shame when she thought how she had decided that they ought to get married when she was twenty-one. Johnnie had looked at her with eyes which were more serious than usual.

They had been walking home from a New Year's Eve dance. Heather had just passed her eighteenth birthday, with Johnnie three years older. It was a clear, bright night, crisp with frost, and the beauty of Locharin had caught at her heart. How she loved her life here.

She was working at the Maitland Dog Kennels, about two miles along the Brechinbridge road, and Johnnie had started his training as a veterinary surgeon. They had such a lot in common, and Heather had looked up at him with eyes which shone in the moonlight.

I NEVER want to leave Locharin," she said. "I love it so. Don't you, Johnnie?"

She had hardly waited for his reply.

"We could get married and live here for the rest of our lives," she said in the breathless voice which she used when she was excited. "Don't you think we could, Johnnie?"

She could sense the change in him almost immediately and knew that she had startled himi.

"What's the matter?" she asked, laughingly. "Should I have waited for a leap year?"

"Oh, Heather," he said, grasping her hand tightly, "You're such a child yet."

"I'm eighteen. We could be engaged for a little while, though I would want to wear an engagement ring. Just a very small one would do.

"And I'd want a white wedding, even if we only invite our own families. Maybe I'm a bit old fashioned, Johnnie, but that's what I should like for us.

"My experience at the kennels would help you in your work, and I just know we would be happy. I love you, Johnnie. Don't you love me, even a little?"

"More than a little," he said, quickly, though she could sense the constraint in him.

"You don't want to," she said. "You don't feel the same way."

"We'll talk about it another time, Heather," he said quietly. "It would be so easy to make those kind of plans on a night like this, but there are a lot of harsh days to be lived through in life, too. It isn't easy to earn a living here, and Aunt Hannah has spoiled you a little. You've always had everything you want."

"I want a good night kiss," she told him, hardly listening to a word.

He bent to kiss her and she clung to him, kissing him fiercely, showing her deep love for him.

"Aunt Hannah will be watching from the window," he said, hoarsely. "Better go in now, Heather. Good night, dear."

" 'Night, Johnnie darling," she said happily. "We *are* engaged, aren't we?"

"Maybe," he said, cautiously. "We'll talk it over tomorrow."

NEXT day was New Year's Day and there was an air of excitement, renewal and out-going love in the small community of Locharin.

Johnnie called to first-foot Aunt Hannah, and Heather rushed downstairs in her new russet-brown suit which she had kept specially for this occasion.

"Well?" she asked.

Johnnie's eyes were bright as he looked at her, then he nodded.

"If that's what you want."

"Oh, Johnnie!" she said. "Of course it's what I want."

"It's just that . . . you've lived here since you were five, and you've never known anywhere else. You went straight to the kennels after school, yet . . . yet you were born in London and your mother's people were Londoners. You might grow restless when you are a little older.

"I don't want you to rush into anything, Heather. We'll choose a ring, but I want us to wait till I'm fully qualified before we marry. I want to give you what you might have had, if only . . . if only things had been different for you. I've seen great unhappiness among my own friends, if decisions are made lightly."

"But this is what I want, Johnnie."

"It's what you *think* you want. You always leap into things too quickly. Locharin is a slow place."

"My father was born here, and I take after him in nature. Besides, Aunt Hannah brought me up, so I'm Locharin through and through."

Johnnie looked at her searchingly, then he bent to kiss her.

"We'll go to Edinburgh for the ring," he promised her. "Soon."

Heather had expected Aunt Hannah to be overjoyed at the news of her engagement. But the older woman had looked at her with searching eyes before kissing her warmly and turning to shake Johnnie's hand.

"Johnnie says we have to wait," Heather told her.

"It will give me time to make a housewife of you," Aunt Hannah told her. "Otherwise he'll be eating a dog's dinner every night."

"Not to mention a dog's breakfast every morning," Heather returned, her eyes full of mischief.

Looking back over the past two years, Heather realised, now, just how young she had been.

She had been so sure that Johnnie shared her own happiness. Yet she had known how difficult he found it to express his feelings. Even when they were children and she had learned that if anything was "all right," then it was giving him a great deal of pleasure, and "very nice" meant that he was looking on true beauty. He rarely spoke endearments to her, but she listened to the love in his voice, whenever he spoke her name.

His father was an equally quiet man who looked at her with kindly eyes, and his mother was one of Aunt Hannah's oldest friends. Sometimes they both looked at her searchingly when she bought a new disc which she had admired on "Top Of The Pops" and laughed heartily at the expression on Aunt Hannah's face as she danced to the music. Neither of the ladies appreciated the music Heather loved.

It was partly because of this music that her life became so shattered a few months after her engagement. She was playing records in her room one afternoon and didn't realise that Mrs McBride had called to see Aunt Hannah.

She was getting ready for an evening out with Johnnie when she remembered that her favourite lipstick was in her handbag downstairs. Softly, she padded down in her stocking feet.

She paused as she heard Mrs McBride's voice.

So You Think You Know About Ireland?

1. Who presented himself as Emperor of Ireland in 1005?
2. What is the Black Pig's Race?
3. Where would you find Finn Mac Cool's Quoits and what are they?
4. What is the name of the annual festival for which Killorglin, County Kerry, is famous?

Answers below.

1. Brian Boru.
2. An ancient frontier earthwork built in the 3rd century.
3. At the foot of Carrigmor, Howth. They are a prehistoric chamber tomb.
4. Aonach an Phuic (Poc Fair).

"I tell you, Hannah, I don't know what to think. Our Johnnie won't talk about it. Maybe he's got himself into a corner he can't get out of, and he's too kind to risk hurting Heather.

"Maybe there's nothing to worry about, of course, but I feel he's not a hundred per cent. sure about this engagement."

HEATHER stopped abruptly in her tracks.

Aunt Hannah sighed before she spoke in reply. "Oh, Nell, I'm sure that Johnnie wouldn't do anything foolish, even to please Heather.

"I know she's very young and I wish I could be sure that she knows what she wants. Sometimes she seems so contented here, then I can see her desire for a more . . . more modern way of life bubbling in her. If Johnnie senses this in her . . . well . . . if he loves her enough . . ."

"Ah, but does he?" Johnnie's mother asked.

"He's always looked on her as his wee sister. I just don't know if he loves her differently now, or if she loves him as a woman should. I think that's the trouble, Hannah. What do you think? Is she mature enough . . ."

Heather didn't wait to hear any more. Hurriedly, she padded back to

132

her room, and sat down at her dressing-table. Her throat burned with tears as she stared back at the white face she saw in the mirror.

Johnnie loved her! He did! He loved her!

She clenched her hands and wanted to shout it to the rooftops. She wanted to rush downstairs and tell Mrs McBride that she was all wrong. Aunt Hannah, too. She was truly in love with Johnnie, as a woman should be. In fact, she had enough love in her for two . . .

The thought was like a douche of cold water. Was that what had happened? Perhaps she *had* enough love in her for two!

Her eyes grew big and dark as she began to remember that it was she who had proposed to Johnnie. But that was only because it was always she who suggested what they ought to do with their time! Tonight they were going dancing, for instance. But did Johnnie really *want* to go dancing? Or had he only agreed to do what she wanted?

She had felt warmed by his protective love but now she began to wonder if it was his great kindness and warm-heartedness which he had to offer, and not love.

HEATHER felt she had grown much older as she and Johnnie drove over to the dance at Brechinbridge. Soon he was teasing her about being quiet, and not the other way round.

"I want to talk to you, Johnnie," she told him. "Let's walk outside for a while."

"Just as we did the night we got engaged," he said, smiling.

"The night I was brazen enough to propose marriage to you," she said in a low voice. "You really *didn't* want to be tied down to an engagement, did you, Johnnie?" she asked. "I . . . I realise it now. You were only humouring me."

His eyes grew watchful. "What's brought this on, Heather?"

"Oh . . . just that I didn't realise at the time what . . . well . . . how I might have been making things difficult for you and . . . and myself, too."

"Why are you suddenly thinking like this?"

She could not tell him about her eavesdropping, and she avoided looking at him.

"Perhaps I am older now," she said quietly. "Perhaps I want it to be up to you. If you want to call it off then you only have to say so. I rushed things, didn't I? Perhaps I rushed things for my own good. It was wrong of me."

Again she felt his scrutiny and steeled herself to meet it. It was up to Johnnie now. If he wanted her he must be the one to persuade her.

"I won't hold you to anything, Heather." Again there was restraint in him as he stared at her. "I only want you to be happy. Do you want to try your wings after all? Is that what you are trying to tell me?"

She wanted to deny it, but she could not read his thoughts.

"I think so," she said, testing him again. "How do you really feel about it, Johnnie?"

He smiled gently. "It's all right, dear, I'll let you go. There's no real harm done. I didn't realise you were so restless, but that's because I've been very busy lately. Men in my profession don't pay enough attention to those closest to them. I'm sorry, Heather."

She was sure that there was relief in his voice, and he was certainly talking much more than he usually did. Pride flamed in her again.

"I want to go to London," she said. "I want to see where I was born."

SURPRISINGLY, Heather loved London once she had settled down. Her experience gained her a good position in a busy surgery for sick animals and she became a "third girl" in a small flat.

She met Simon Watson at a party and found his company exciting and stimulating.

When she came back home to Locharin, Johnnie was in practice at Brechinbridge and she saw nothing of him. Neither did she notice Aunt Hannah looked so frail until it was too late.

Now Heather was alone, except for Simon who wanted to marry her. She had promised to give him her answer after she had arranged the sale of Aunt Hannah's house. She had seen Johnnie at the funeral, but there had been no opportunity to talk.

One or two of Aunt Hannah's pieces of furniture were going to a saleroom in Edinburgh and Heather wandered into the garden, not wishing to see them being moved. When she returned to the house, the removal man handed her an old photograph. "It was down the back of that sideboard."

After they had gone, Heather looked at the school photograph, the lump in her throat now dissolving into tears.

She remembered it well. She and Johnnie had both owned a copy, but one copy had disappeared and Heather claimed the survivor.

FULL CIRCLE

CHRISTMAS would be so different for Mary. Now she had been to Bethlehem. Heard its deep-voiced bells. Viewed the airless cavern they call the stable, out-by the howe of the plains.

Home she brought a pocketful of memories and a wad of snaps.

Now Christmas Eve was approaching. Poor substitute her country kirk for Bethlehem's pillared hall!

Then came the gale. The roof was ripped, the church was closed.

"Where shall we hold Christmas?" they cried.

Spoke up Mains himself, "In my auld stable where once stood sax pair!"

All lent a hand. Such scrubbing, such preparing.

So with accordion for music and bales for pews, by lantern light they kept tryst with Christmas Eve. In their stable "Kirk"!

"Better even than Bethlehem," Mary confessed.
Rev. T. R. S. Campbell.

For once Johnnie had protested. "No, that's mine, Heather. Yours had a wee red mark on the back."

"It did not! This is mine. I put it on the table."

"No, I did. It's mine. I don't know where yours is."

Finally Johnnie had parted with the photograph and Heather's tears turned to smiles.

Now she looked at the one with the small red mark on the back and knew that she could never marry Simon. It was Johnnie she loved and always had.

Neither could she part with Aunt Hannah's house.

Aunt Hannah had lived quite happily by herself and so could she. Here her heart might ache for Johnnie, but at least he would not be far away. She could see him, even if he did not love her in the same way.

With renewed energy, Heather began the long task of setting the house to rights. It felt as though Aunt Hannah were still with her, watching her with pleasure and perhaps a little curiosity.

"I tried spreading my wings, Aunt Hannah," she said, aloud, "but my heart is here. It always was and always will be."

"I hope you mean that, Heather," Johnnie said from the doorway.

She turned to him, her heart leaping with shock.

"I didn't hear you coming in." They stared at one another and she could only read love in his eyes. This time there was no restraint in him.

"Johnnie?" she asked.

"Somehow I always felt you would come back," he said, "and I would be waiting, however long it took.

"I wanted you to have your chance, my darling. You seemed so young to make your choice before, and if it had been the wrong one you might have been unhappy. I had to be sure that you were sure, but I would have waited a lifetime for you, Heather, because I love you."

"Well, you almost lost me, Johnnie McBride," she said, going into his arms. "I was coming to return this photograph to you. After this, we'll have to decide more carefully who is right and who is wrong. You are far too fond of giving me my own way!" □

OUT OF THE

FRYING PAN!

by MARY LEDGWAY

AILEEN EVERLEY looked round the small, but comfortably-furnished room at Elm Lodge with a feeling of relief. At last her holiday had begun and she was free from sympathetic glances, from friends dragging her to parties, determined to find her someone to take Rodney's place.

How do you convince people who care about you that although Rodney made the break, she soon found she was quite happy without him? Oh, she didn't deny that those months with Rodney had held something special, expensive theatre seats, candlelit dinners. Once he had gone out of her life, though, it was just a pleasant period to look back on.

True, her pride had been dented a little, but she was certainly not hiding the bruised heart her friends seemed to expect.

Mrs Dalby, the motherly landlady, served her an ample cold tea.

"Cold on Saturdays, love. People coming all hours and they're ready for something when they get here.

"And what are you planning for tonight?" she asked as she cleared the table.

It was only just after six o'clock. The long, hot day was all ready to spill over into the evening.

"I'd like to swim," Aileen told her. "But the beach looked a bit tatty when I came through."

"Oh, that middle bit always does! If you want a nice swim, love, get the number twelve bus to Beggin's Way. It's only a short walk to the beach and there's a natural pool there. Fills up with the tide and not many people know about it. Mind you let that meal settle first!"

Mrs Dalby was right. The pool was almost deserted. Aileen floated in the warm, salt water. Granted, she cast a few longing glances at the sea, where the white horses were rolling in with ever-increasing force, but the beach was almost empty and commonsense told her not to go in alone. After her swim she lay on the rocks a while, then, in the cool of the evening, walked slowly back to Elm Lodge.

The next day Aileen found herself sharing a table at lunch with Lorna Greensmith, a pleasant woman in her mid-thirties. Aileen liked her on sight.

"I come here several times a year," Lorna told her. "I have an aunt in a home about twelve miles away. So I come here for a few days and visit at the same time."

Lorna said she was going to walk along the front after lunch.

"There's a farmhouse and they make the most delicious cream teas. I know we don't need them, with Mrs Dalby's cooking, but I don't think a bit of spoiling now and again does any harm. Why not come with me?"

Aileen enjoyed her afternoon. There was a welcome breeze on the

137

cliff top, and the farmhouse tea was all Lorna promised. It was time for dinner when they arrived back, and, tired with the sea air, they spent a lazy evening in the lounge.

THE following day Lorna was going to visit her aunt. Aileen decided to go back to Beggin's Way for another swim. There were not many people there, a few sunbathers on the rocks, and one or two swimmers.

For a time Aileen joined the sunbathers, but after a while, she let her eyes rest on the gently lapping sea. The ripples of foam were softer than before. They caressed the shore with a soft, gentle rhythm. Aileen stood up and began to make her way down to the beach.

"No!"

Aileen turned in surprise.

"I wouldn't — I mean, it isn't really safe."

The speaker was a bronzed young man Aileen had already seen lying on the rocks, and she had noticed he made no effort to swim. When he stood up, he towered over her. Suddenly all her old irritation at people trying to run her life returned.

"Surely if it were that bad there would be warning notices? Anyway —" She smiled with exaggerated sweetness — "I'm sure if I get into difficulties a big handsome man like you would save me!"

He shook his head.

"I'm quite sure you've already noticed I keep clear of the water," he told her.

Because she had, she felt more annoyed than ever. "Well, if you can't swim — don't try to stop those who can."

He shrugged, and walked back to the rocks.

Aileen turned away, but not far enough to prevent her seeing him gather up his towel and stroll out of sight.

After he had gone, her bravado faded away. She felt ashamed. The tart rejoinders were not like her, and she knew her remarks had bordered on rudeness.

She looked at the sea, calm, inviting. If he couldn't swim, he couldn't really know, she persuaded herself.

Carefully, she waded in, then struck out, lazily riding the white horses.

But the stranger's words had gone home. Soon Aileen put her feet down and found she could only just reach the sandy bottom. That alone would not have alarmed her, for she was a good swimmer; but she also felt the pull of conflicting currents.

Turning, she found it took all her efforts to make her way to the shore, where she flopped on to the sand, too tired even to make her way the extra few yards to her towel, spread on the rocks.

Again her thoughts went to the stranger. She knew that if it had not been for his warning she would have swum farther out before turning back. She shuddered as she thought of the possible consequences.

Rested, she made her way back to where she had left her clothes. Once dressed she looked at the local map Mrs Dalby had lent her.

Out Of The Frying Pan!

Having had enough of the sea, Aileen decided to make her way inland and took the bus to Tiburton, a pretty village with white-washed cottages and a stream.

Still feeling shaken, she sat outside a cottage café and had tea and scones. The tea helped and soon she felt better. After all, no harm had come to her, and she had learned a lesson. If only she hadn't been so rude to the unknown man . . .

THE afternoon passed pleasantly. Aileen found a local craft centre and watched nimble fingers turning pots, weaving the local sheep's wool. She saw glass engraving and china painting. It was just what she needed to distract her mind from what had happened, and by the time she got back to Elm Lodge, she was her old self.

Lorna was just about to pick up the telephone. They smiled at each other. In spite of the difference in ages, they both knew they would remain friends, keeping in touch with each other.

"I'm just going to ring up and book for the Aqua Show," Lorna told her. "Like to come?"

"Love to," Aileen said promptly.

They caught the bus to town and found they had good seats in the front row. Aileen looked round eagerly. It was her first visit to an Aqua Show, although Lorna said she came every year. The swimming pool was decorated with garlands of flowers and colourful drapes, and it was cool and pleasant after the heat outside.

The first half opened with the Flower Swimmers, a delightful group who performed magical things in the water. Their swim caps were made of flowers, and they had flowers in their hands, on their feet. The patterns they formed and their graceful movements in perfect unison were enchanting.

They were followed by trapeze artists and tightrope walkers. Then Dan's Daring Divers were announced. The lights were dimmed and when they came on again the divers were grouped on the high diving board.

Aileen looked up, straight into the eyes of the man on the beach. His amused smile told her he had recognised her, and she felt herself blushing, remembering her curt rejection of his warning.

" 'Dan's Daring Divers' will now entertain you," he announced.

His salute embraced the whole audience, but Aileen felt the last mocking wave was for her alone. She would have liked to muster up enough courage to walk out, but knew she really wanted to watch, to see Dan diving.

Soon Aileen was watching breathlessly as they hurled themselves into the water — single, double, treble somersaults, diving in pairs, in threes.

The applause was tumultuous, and Aileen groaned to herself as she remembered how she had taunted Dan about not swimming.

Fun and frolics was the next item. Clowns ran hither and thither. Tramps fell in the pool, clambered out and were pushed in again. The children laughed and cheered. Finally the troupe ran round, throwing balloons and flowers to the audience, who caught them delightedly.

Aileen was taken by surprise when a flower landed right in her lap. The thrower laughed up at her. Behind the painted face of the clown, her "beach boy," as she had come to think of him, was easily recognised. He blew her a kiss, and ran off.

Aileen picked up the flower and found a note attached with an elastic band. *Coffee at Michael's café, tomorrow, 11 a.m. Please!* she read.

The note was still in her hand when the lights went up for the interval. Lorna looked at it and grinned.

So You Think You Know About England?

1. Which children's author lived at Sawrey, in the Lake District?
2. Which Yorkshire seaside town is famous for jet?
3. Where in the South of England would the Devil find his Punchbowl?
4. What West Country town is the real Casterbridge in Thomas Hardy's novels?
5. Which city has a greater mileage of canals than Venice?
6. Who is the Warden of the Cinque Ports?

Answers below.

6. *The Queen Mother.*
5. *Birmingham.*
4. *Dorchester.*
3. *Surrey.*
2. *Whitby.*
1. *Beatrix Potter.*

"A fast worker," she teased.

"Well, we have met," admitted Aileen. "I'll tell you later. Fancy an ice-cream?" she asked, to change the subject.

She pushed the note out of sight in her bag, but she could not push it out of her mind.

THE second half of the show was much like the first. The comedy was more hilarious, the swimmers, if possible, more graceful than ever in their mermaid costumes, and the diving more daring.

Aileen could read the question in Dan's eyes, but was careful to give no sign of having read the note, to give no indication of acceptance or refusal. She didn't think she could face him again.

On the way home she told Lorna about the meeting on the beach.

"Of course you must go," her friend insisted. "If only to apologise," she added with a grin.

"It's just that I'm rather wary at the moment," Aileen said with a little frown.

"Well, meeting someone for coffee in the middle of the morning hardly constitutes a tremendous risk," Lorna pointed out. "And after all, from what you've just told me, he does deserve an apology."

Out Of The Frying Pan!

L ORNA left for home the following morning, and somewhat nervously, at eleven o'clock, Aileen walked into Michael's café.

Dan, tall and sunburnt, in white shorts and shirt, stood up to greet her.

"First, let me say I'm sorry!" The words rushed out from Aileen. "You were right about the sea. I was rude! I don't really know why. I'm not usually like that."

He pulled out a chair for her and signalled the waiter.

"It was as much my fault," he assured her. "Only during the show period we aren't supposed to swim anywhere but the pool. Something to do with insurance or something," he added vaguely. "I ought to have explained more. I would have come after you, though, only you coped well alone."

She blushed. "You saw me go in then?"

"I was watching from the rocks. Now drink your coffee and tell me what an attractive young lady like you is doing holidaying alone?"

So Aileen found herself telling him about Rodney and her well-meaning friends.

"And there's no heart-ache — not one little bit?"

"No! Although no-one believes me. Now tell me what you are doing in a summer show."

Aileen learned he was a physical education teacher at a large comprehensive school about 30 miles from her home town.

"Swimming and diving has always been my hobby," he told her. "For the last three years I've done the show. It fills the long summer break."

Aileen wondered — was there a slight reserve in his voice? Surely there were other, easier ways to spend his holidays, but he was speaking again.

"How about spending a day on Greansea Island? I've no matinee on Wednesdays so we could have a nice long day. I'm told it's well worth a visit. There's a bird sanctuary and the peacocks are almost tame, so I'm told."

Dan and Aileen caught the early ferry the next morning. They leaned over the rails and the wind blew Aileen's hair. She put her hands up to tidy it, but Dan stopped her.

"Leave it," he told her. "It looks nice windblown."

They had an early lunch near the ferry, then wandered round the island.

There were shady paths between the trees. Crooked tracks led to secluded beaches. They took their sandals off and walked along the edge of tiny ripples. From the cool of shady glens they watched the birds, even a red squirrel showed itself.

Then, reaching the far end of the island, they sat down on the soft turf. Dan opened his rucksack and drew out a flask.

"Cider," he said. "Hope you like it. Cider, sandwiches and fruit."

They ate contentedly. The cider was ice cold, and they fed the crusts to two peacocks, who came and took the food out of their hands, strolling away when the food was finished.

Aileen lay back, the sun warm on her face, her heart light. Her

141

thoughts drifted back to Rodney. He would have hated a day like this, away from civilisation, but she felt only a deep contentment.

Aileen didn't try to analyse her feelings, not letting her thoughts extend beyond this perfect day. Dan had said little about his past — perhaps there was someone else, perhaps not. For the moment Aileen was happy, relaxing in this gentle place. Here was peace — tranquillity . . .

DAN was quietly conscious of the girl beside him. How long since he had enjoyed a day like today? His thoughts turned to that day in the Easter holidays, three years before.

Sheila! How he had loved her. He was all ready to go out and meet her when the telephone call came.

"It's Auntie! She's not well, Dan. I can't leave her."

"I'll come over," he offered.

"No, please don't! I'm sure she'd rather be quiet."

So he spent the day preparing work for school, until the phone rang again.

Sheila was still unconscious when he reached the hospital.

"A motor-bike," the doctor explained. "She was riding pillion. We got your address from a letter in her bag."

Sheila recovered, but his faith in women was shattered. He had been so sure she loved him, that he could trust her. If she had been honest, told him there was someone else — but she hadn't wanted to give up the things he could give her, or the excitement she derived from her other friend.

It was then Dan looked round for something to fill the summer break. The show came along and it had served to fill time in ever since. He had almost forgotten Sheila now but it had made him steer clear of other girls, other attachments.

Until he met a girl on the sands, a girl with defiant blue eyes, and enough spirit or foolhardiness to ignore a warning. She was a girl who could share a day on a small island and give that day a magical quality.

One day he would tell her about Sheila, when the time was right, but for now he would just relax, enjoy the peace — and tranquillity . . .

JOHN O' GROATS

Contrary to belief, John o' Groats is not the most northerly point of mainland Britain, this distinction properly belonging to nearby Dunnet Head. The name comes from a Dutchman, John de Groot, who settled here in the late 15th century and who, with his two brothers, ran a ferry to South Ronaldsay in the Orkneys. A mound with a flagstaff near the hotel marks the site of the unusual house he built for his eight descendants. He designed an octagonal house with eight doors, so that each man could say he had his own door. Not content with that, he built an octagonal table so that there was no "head" of the table.

JOHN O' GROATS

SLOWLY I rounded the bend in the road. Then, as I knew I would, I
pulled the car on to the grass verge, switched off the engine and
just looked.

Below me the narrow gorge I'd been following opened out into a wide
sweep of valley. Today, in early February, mist shrouded the dip in a
white blanket of mystery. An occasional gust of wind stirred the
cloudlike surface, sending a ripple of movement among the dead fronds
on the opposite bank. Below me, on the descending slope, there was a
slight stirring through the clumps of grasses that had survived the
winter.

I leaned back and closed my eyes, seeing the valley as it was that
golden summer day.

I saw the smooth white boulders, that divided the river as it gushed
from the gorge . . . Then the two tranquil stretches of gently-flowing
water . . . I saw the children playing, heard their laughter and the
occasional shouted warning from an anxious parent.

144

A World Apart

by Mary Shepherd

I saw two young people, a boy and a girl scrambling through waist-high bracken on the opposite bank. I remembered how I stumbled and I remembered the feel of Trevor's hand as he pulled me over the rough patches . . . a strong, guiding hand.

Then we were on the path and I was brushing bits of heather and fronds of fern from my jeans. I ran my fingers through my hair, wishing I had a comb.

Trevor smiled down at me. "You look fine, Lynne. Come on! We haven't any time to waste if we want to enjoy our tea."

So we ran along the rutted path. When we came to the road, we still ran, so that we arrived at the farm laughing, and breathless.

"Gracious!" Molly Jefferson, the farmer's wife, greeted us. "What a rush some people are in."

"Well, I remembered your famous teas." Trevor smiled. "We decided we just had time. We've to catch the coach back from the cricket pavilion at seven."

"Right! Sit down and drink this. I'll call you when it's ready."

So we sat on a bench overlooking the farmyard and the fields, and drank ice-cold lemonade.

We'd come to this little village in the Yorkshire Dales to support our town's cricket team. They needed all the encouragement they could get and we always made sure all the empty seats in the coach were filled.

Trevor and I had known each other for as long as I could remember, but only I knew how often I thought about him. Only I knew the dreams I dreamed.

Neither of us were cricket fans, so when Trevor mentioned he knew a spot by the river where we could sit in the sun, I went willingly. We left the others to their game and sat on a boulder with our feet in the stream.

Suddenly Trevor handed me a large handkerchief. "Come on — put those shoes on, it's time to move!"

I glanced at my watch. "But —"

"I know a farmhouse along the tops — Dad took us there last year and the farmer's wife does a lovely tea. If we cut up the bank we'll just have time."

"But I haven't any money!" I protested.

He grinned. "I have. Enough for both of us. I did some gardening and saved up. I just knew we were going to have a super day today."

A S we sat sipping the lemonade I thought of an old story I had read. One that insisted everyone has a magic day during their lifetime. If that is true, I thought, this is mine — my own magic day.

On the bench Trevor's fingers were just touching mine. I sat, not daring to move, afraid of breaking that slender link.

All too soon Mrs Jefferson called us in. The plates were piled high with ham, eggs, mushrooms and tomatoes. A crusty loaf on a wooden platter and deep yellow butter. There were large cups and a huge brown tea-pot.

"I'll hack the loaf while you pour the tea." Trevor laughed as he picked up the knife.

As I lifted the heavy pot and poured the rich brown liquid into Trevor's cup, so much happiness flooded through me that it almost hurt. I wondered how one small body could contain so much.

But as Trevor handed me slices of home-made bread covered with fresh butter, I found that happiness was no hindrance to eating, whatever the poets said about it.

We finished off with apple pie, chunks of fruit cake and cheese.

"I don't know how we're going to walk back." Trevor laughed as he paid Mrs Jefferson a surprisingly small sum for such a large meal.

"You don't have to. My man is taking some hay to another farm along that way. You can have a lift up if you like."

So we sat on the hay as the cart trundled over the bridge and along the road. This time Trevor's hand covered mine and I wished the journey could last for ever.

That summer we spent a lot of time together. Shyly we began to talk, to get to know each other. We held hands and exchanged our first gentle kisses. We didn't make plans. We were young, there was plenty of time; sufficient for us that the sun shone, that we were strong and healthy.

Trevor persuaded me to buy some walking boots and we tramped the countryside. We'd climb far above the haunts of tourists into the hills, to picnic near smooth, dark-deep tarns, or in the shelter of the woods, or by a brook, its gentle ripple vying with the birds' songs for purity of sound.

Suddenly the summer was over.

It was September as Trevor left for university. I went back to my last year at school and was soon caught up in class affairs and studying for my "A"-levels. I stored up scraps of news for Trevor, but he was not a good letter writer. I began to cut down on mine to him, afraid of appearing too eager, too clinging.

Then Christmas came, and with it Trevor. My world was right again.

We joined the carol singers, and though we were both with our own families at the midnight service, our eyes met and I knew that the old magic, for me anyway, was still there.

I gave Trevor a pullover, painstakingly knitted in my spare time. He gave me a pencil sketch he had asked one of his fellow students to do for him. It was of a table, laden with a farmhouse tea. In the corner the hands of a girl were just visible as she poured from the huge brown pot.

Trevor had put it in a plain white frame and I stood it near my bed. My heart was warm as I realised that he, too, treasured memories of that day.

Then, early in the New Year the blow fell. Trevor's father had to choose between redundancy and a move to the South, about as far away from our little Yorkshire town as it could be. Of course, he chose to work — so before the Easter holiday came round there were new people in the house across the town.

Trevor didn't come up for Easter.

I can't come, Lynne, he wrote. *There's such a lot to be done to the new house. I have to help.*

I consoled myself with the thought that summer was near. Then Trevor took a holiday job and I had the chance of work at a firm of solicitors. I didn't dare refuse; such jobs were scarce. Unfortunately it meant that when Trevor was free, I wasn't.

WE did meet in October. Trevor wrote that a group of students were going to a youth hostel for an activity weekend. He suggested we got a small party together and met up.

It was not a success.

Trevor's group were tackling rock climbing far beyond anything I could do. One of the other students, Debby, was seldom far from his side, and I found myself harbouring a growing resentment. Later, when I looked back, I realised I had never seen Trevor seek her out, or give her any encouragement.

Only on our last night, when we were sitting round the huge wood fire, did we come anywhere near our old intimacy. He asked about my work and told me about the new life his parents were making for themselves. I talked back, taking refuge in a flippancy I didn't feel to mask my feelings.

The buzz of surrounding conversation drowned our whispers and Trevor leaned across.

"Lynne! What's wrong, love? What is it?"

"Nothing's wrong. I've had a lovely weekend."

"I don't mean the weekend! I mean us. I thought we were friends — special friends."

"We are — but we're both older," I said, conjuring up a laugh. "And wiser," I added, unable to hide a touch of bitterness despite myself.

Debby had come over, probably resenting our private conversation. I stood up to give her my seat, regretting my action as I glanced back and saw Trevor laughing over some remark of hers.

Upstairs I curled up in my sleeping bag and let the tears come, glad of the privacy of my top bunk. When the others came up I feigned sleep.

The next morning I was up early, determined to talk to Trevor. I'd made up my mind to sink my pride and try to close the rift that was widening between us.

His group were already preparing to leave when I found him. There was only time for the briefest of goodbyes before waving him away.

It was soon after this that James Grant came into the office.

He wanted the junior partner who was out, so I made him coffee and he sat in my office waiting. The senior clerk, who shared the office, was at lunch, and as I typed I felt embarrassed by the admiration in his eyes.

I stopped to put a new sheet of paper in my typewriter and he took advantage of the lull.

"I thought solicitors' offices were full of musty books and hard-bitten tyrants." He laughed. "Not pretty girls."

I smiled and began to type again.

"I'm sure part of your duties is to keep clients happy," he intervened.

This time I laughed.

"I wouldn't know. I haven't been here long and don't usually meet the clients." But I took my hands off the keys and picked up my coffee.

"That's better!" James Grant leaned back in his chair and began to ask me about the town.

He travelled a lot in his job, but he'd just bought a flat because he wanted a settled base of his own to come back to.

SOON James and I were dating regularly. He was practically the opposite of Trevor and shuddered at the sight of a pair of walking boots.

When James was home my spare time became a round of theatres, concerts and meals out. When he was away I found myself looking forward to his return. I was the envy of my friends. He was handsome, good company and generous. He planned our time and I was content to let him.

Christmas came round again and Trevor sent me a book on the Lake District. As I glanced through the maps and sketches, read the words which conjured up visions of green fells and snow-topped hills, I felt a wave of nostalgia for my old way of life. I yearned to put my boots on and set off to tramp the hills; to sit in the shelter of an old stone wall, eating sandwiches and drinking piping-hot coffee from the flask. I missed that wild and lonely world, a world I knew with Trevor, a world so few of us are privileged to ever know.

I put the book on the shelf and slipped into my new evening dress, a present from my parents. James' gift of a small diamond drop looked perfect as I fastened it round my throat.

As I walked to James' car, the snow flakes fell softly, on to my fur jacket. I looked back and saw the tiny imprints of my high-heeled dance shoes in the light covering of snow. I was a different girl now.

I was almost 21 when James asked me to marry him. I said yes, sure that what I felt for him would grow into something deeper. By then I'd convinced myself that my feelings for Trevor had only been a young girl's growing pains.

As the wedding day grew nearer, I waited for the bells of happiness to start ringing. They were silent.

Then one evening as James and I were going into my home, Trevor was coming out.

"Hello, Lynne!" He smiled, but the smile didn't light his soft grey eyes. They were closed, shuttered; I couldn't read them.

"Your mother tells me congratulations are in order. You must be James. You're a lucky man. Look after her . . ."

He brushed my cheek with a gentle, lingering finger. Then he was striding away from me, out of my life.

Suddenly I knew that if I never saw Trevor again, I could still not belong to anyone else.

James seemed more angry than hurt when I told him. I knew he would soon find consolation elsewhere.

And me? I dug out my walking boots, and disobeying all the rules, trudged away on my own, over the hills and fells, discovering tiny, hidden valleys and streams.

What A Celebration!

THE cheese straws have no cheese in,
　I'm out of sparkling wine,
One guest has phoned to cancel,
　But really things are fine!
Oh, now I've smudged my lipstick,
　And lost an earring, too,
Can't think who I invited —
　A really mixed who's who!
I'll try this soda syphon,
　It has a funny quirk —
Like being slow to function,
　So will it really work?
Oh dear! It's drenched the table,
　And every savoury,
So what a celebration
　This non-event will be!
Elizabeth Gozney.

I ROAMED the high tops every weekend I could, revelling in the space and the solitude. The weather smiled on me, and I developed a routine of getting up early on Saturday morning and packing my rucksack with the essentials — food, coffee, waterproofs and maps.

I felt a curious sense of peace, of emerging from a maelstrom of artificial gaiety to quiet calm.

Not till October, when I was caught alone in a sudden mist, did I acknowledge the dangers. Fortunately I was able to get back to the road, but the experience frightened me, and I joined a local walking group.

That winter we went for miles, in the sun, the rain and the snow. We loved the open spaces, the freedom, and the feeling of fighting the elements. It didn't matter what the weather was like — we literally took it in our stride.

I joined in the social side of the group, too, and went away with them. But I fought shy of any attachment. At least, I felt I was coming to terms with life.

Then Trevor's aunt died. Because I had known her all my life, and she had shown me many kindnesses, I went to the church. But I sat at the back, determined to avoid Trevor if he was there.

He was waiting for me. He picked up my left hand. "So you changed your mind?"

I hurried home. With the money I had saved for my wedding I had bought a small car. I got in and drove away. Away from more hurt — away from Trevor.

When I got back Mother said he had called.

"He left you this." She sounded puzzled.

"This" was a teapot from a child's teaset. It had once been bright blue, but now it boasted a quick coat of brown enamel. So he had remembered.

I smiled and felt my cheeks wet with tears . . .

A ND now here I was, the following day, with the brown teapot on the car seat beside me, and the road to the dales stretching ahead.

I drove on, looking for the bridge the hay cart had trundled across, with its two young hitch-hikers on the back. In a few minutes I was at the farm asking Mrs Jefferson if there was any chance of a cup of tea.

"Come on in, lassie! You look frozen!" This time there was a huge fire blazing in the hearth, but the room was empty.

My heart sank. I'd been wrong after all.

"It's a good meal you'll be wanting — that's for sure!"

I sat back as she bustled about setting the table. I closed my eyes and the warmth of the fire lulled my senses.

Faintly I smelt the aroma of frying ham, then suddenly the light was blocked out as two strong hands covered my eyes.

"Guess who?"

I didn't have to. Without hesitation I loosened one of the hands and pressed it to my lips.

"Lynne! Oh, Lynne! Why have we wasted all this time?" Trevor asked as he pulled me from the depths of the chair into his arms. But I was content to let explanations wait.

Hand in hand we walked across to the laden table.

"You hack the bread," I said softly. "I'll pour the tea."

Once again I lifted the heavy brown teapot. Again I poured the tea — but this time I knew I would go on pouring the tea. This time the bells of happiness were ringing loud and clear.

As my eyes met Trevor's, the years between fell away. Together we laughed and began to eat. □

ONCE YOU HAVE FOUND HIM

by
GRACE
MACAULAY

A S soon as she woke, she heard the patter of rain. She sat up and gazed out the window incredulously, stupidly.

It hadn't rained for five weeks and three days. The whole area was suffering from a severe drought. Water had been rationed for over a week now.

She lay back. The garden would welcome the rain. The flowers would brighten. The grass would grow green again. Her father would be able to wash his car. Her mother would be able to wash all the windows.

Linda Kershaw tried to hold on to these positive, happy thoughts, but already there was a tear trickling down her face. She rubbed her eyes fiercely, ashamed to be giving way to such a juvenile reaction.

She had known all along that the summer weather could not last indefinitely. But why, oh why, couldn't it have lasted for just one more day?

Inside her closed eyelids there was a picture of Euan Forbes, looking at her with that charming half-smile which had the power to dazzle and bemuse her. While in her head she heard the vibrant murmur of his deep voice, softened and sweetened for her ear alone.

"We'll take a picnic up to the Corbies' Den, tomorrow, shall we? Just the two of us."

And her own voice, low and tremulous — and stilled when his lips found hers again.

The memory of their kisses caused her heart to soar with rapture — even as she opened her eyes again and watched the raindrops on the window.

"Come on, Lazybones!" her mother called to her. "Your breakfast is ready."

Linda got out of bed at once, but she didn't answer. She didn't want her mother to hear the tears in her voice.

She slipped on her dressing-gown and pushed her feet into her slippers, sniffling childishly as she hurried towards the bathroom.

She was drying her face when her mother called up to her again. This time she was able to reply. "On my way, Mum!"

Her disappointment had not lessened any, but she had it under control now. She certainly wasn't about to let the whole world see her aching heart.

"Sorry, Mum." She even managed a little smile with her apology as she sat down at the breakfast table.

"I should think so, too," Mrs Kershaw told her grumpily. "I've better things to do than wait about all day for you to come down for your breakfast."

L INDA said nothing. There was no point. They both knew that she was perfectly capable of getting her own breakfast, and indeed she normally did.

No, she could guess that her mother was irritable with her because she was in a bad mood about something else. All Linda had to do was wait and she would be told the reason. Mrs Kershaw was like that. When something upset her, she didn't bottle up her feelings.

Maybe that's why I'm so quiet, Linda reflected, as she poured milk on to her porridge. Maybe my reserved nature is caused by 19 years of watching my mother rant and rage about the least little thing. She wondered, rather drearily, what it would be this time.

Mrs Kershaw made a fresh pot of tea and sat down at the table sighing gustily. She did not speak.

The silence lengthened and after a while, Linda stole a glance at her mother's face. She was astonished to see an expression of deep melancholy.

"What's the matter, Mum?" Her question was more of an exclamation of concern. She had never seen her mother looking so sad.

Mrs Kershaw looked at her in a startled kind of way. "What do you mean?"

"Well . . ." Linda scarcely knew how to answer. She felt as if she were invading her mother's privacy. "I only meant . . . why are you so gloomy this morning? I thought something had happened."

Lowering her brows in annoyance, Mrs Kershaw nodded her head in the direction of the window. "Don't tell me you haven't noticed that it's raining."

Catching at her bottom lip with her teeth, Linda held her breath for a moment before she said in a small voice, "I thought you would be pleased."

"And so I am," Mrs Kershaw snapped.

Then after a pause, she added, "At least I ought to be pleased. We've all been waiting and praying for the drought to end, haven't we?"

Linda's mouth twisted wryly. "I suppose so — I hadn't thought." Her mother wasn't really paying attention to her answer. She was watching the rain. "You tend to forget just how depressing a grey sky can be," she said musingly. "You take the blue skies and sunshine for granted. And when you pray for rain — it's a pleasant little shower you are hoping for, not a deluge."

She reached for the teapot, adding more briskly, "Still, it's not as if it's the Great Flood. It's not the end of the world."

"Maybe not for you . . ." Linda hadn't meant to say the words aloud. She would have given anything to be able to call them back as her mother stared at her questioningly.

Linda gulped and tears filled her eyes. "It's Euan's last day . . . we were going on a picnic." She lowered her head quickly, hiding her face.

But her mother had seen. "Oh dear, that's a pity," she said inadequately.

M RS KERSHAW was surprised. She'd had no idea that Linda was so fond of the young holidaymaker who had been taking her out these past few weeks.

In fact, she had understood that Linda was simply making up a foursome with Marion Scott and the other boy. Both lads were staying at Mrs Scott's guest house — she'd an idea that it was originally Mrs Scott who had roped Linda in to help entertain them.

Treading delicately, for her daughter hated to be questioned, Mrs Kershaw said, "A picnic is certainly out of the question . . . unless the weather clears."

Linda gave a small, eloquent shrug. They both knew that the rain wasn't likely to go off.

Mrs Kershaw realised her daughter didn't want to discuss Euan. Linda obviously preferred to keep her feelings locked up inside her. There was nothing she could do but watch helplessly, hurt by her silence.

Yet, there was another sensation besides the hurt in Mrs Kershaw's mind. There was a strange stirring of an old memory.

"I once bought a pair of green sandals," she said pensively. "High heels, they had, so high I could scarcely totter around my room in them. But I was determined to wear them to the dance in the village hall. Someone had told me that the reason your dad never danced with me was because I was so small."

Linda looked up. "And did he dance with you then?"

Mrs Kershaw shook her head. "No . . . the heel snapped off one of my shoes in the cloakroom. I had to wait until everyone was in the hall, then I sneaked out to walk home in my stocking feet."

Linda tilted her head sympathetically. "What a shame."

Mrs Kershaw nodded absently, her eyes dreamy and far away. She did not continue.

Linda eventually asked, "So did you go back to the dance with other shoes on?"

"No — I just went home and cried for hours. I thought my heart was broken and my life was in ruins. I didn't know until the following day that he didn't dance with anyone else. He just stood and watched the door, waiting for me."

"Who told you?"

"Not him, you may be sure!" Mrs Kershaw replied smartly. "You know what he is like — close as a clam and twice as bashful."

She did not say — like yourself — but Linda obviously heard the comparison in her tone and saw it in her face.

LINDA looked down at her plate, crumbling a piece of toast forlornly. She couldn't help not being an outgoing sort of person; no more could her father. But she wondered how her parents had finally got together when they were such opposites.

She was sure her mother hadn't intended to hurt her — but she had. And now neither knew what to say next.

Finally Mrs Kershaw went on with what she'd been saying.

"He'd been told about my shoe, but I knew he wouldn't mention it. So next time I saw him, I told him how disappointed I'd been. I asked him outright if he'd take me up for a dance next Saturday if my heels weren't very high."

She looked at Linda, adding impressively, "That was a bold way for a girl to talk twenty years ago, you know."

A smile tugged at the corners of Linda's mouth. She thought that as far as she was concerned it would still be bold today!

Mrs Kershaw was watching her face and said, with a sparkle in her eyes, "I couldn't just let the disaster go to waste, now could I?"

Linda's smile widened. "Of course not," she agreed sympathetically.

Mrs Kershaw began to gather up the dishes. "After all," she said, rather indignantly, "disasters are supposed to bring people together."

She paused to look at Linda intently. "What will you do now that your picnic is cancelled?"

Taken aback by the unexpected question, Linda gazed up at her mother. "I don't know . . . I said I'd meet him on the corner at eleven . . ."

"You could bring him back here for a meal," Mrs Kershaw suggested. "Then put on some records."

But Linda was shaking her head, retreating into her shell. "I don't think so . . ." she said, busying herself with helping to clear the table.

"It's all right," Mrs Kershaw told her. "I'll manage the dishes. You go on up and get dressed."

Upstairs in her room, Linda was suddenly sorry that she had rejected her mother's suggestion so quickly. For the first time in years she had felt really close to her, the way she had been when she was a little girl. She was deeply sorry that she had caused a new gulf between them. If only she had been able to reveal her feelings about Euan it would never have happened.

Then she frowned, realising for the first time that her mother must have guessed that she was in love . . . and that was why she had spoken about the green shoes and the beginnings of her own romance.

Once You Have Found Him

While she was dressing, Linda's thoughts were a confused mixture of regret and anticipation. Euan would be going home to Glasgow tomorrow. She might never see him again. For although he had said that he loved her, she had been unable to tell him that she loved him, too.

In her heart, she knew that he had waited and longed to hear her saying the words. Now she knew that she could not let him go without telling him.

LINDA hurried downstairs. As she opened the fridge door, she told her mother shyly, "I've decided to make some sandwiches after all. Even if it's raining — we can still go for a walk and shelter somewhere."

Mrs Kershaw tried to hide her surprise. "You'd better take some hot coffee in the flask," she said after a moment. "Or tea, if you'd rather."

Linda nodded. "I'll take coffee."

She glanced at her mother and said hesitantly, "I know it seems silly . . . a picnic in the rain . . . But you see . . . with it being Euan's last day here . . ." She blushed and looked down, concentrating on spreading butter on a slice of bread.

But Mrs Kershaw understood. "I know, dear," she said softly. "You have things to say to each other and you don't want anyone to intrude, I'm sure."

Impulsively, Linda went over to her and gave her a hug.

"I wish I could tell you more, Mum. But the truth is — I don't know what will be happening with Euan and me." She faltered and her eyes filled with tears. "I mean, he hasn't said anything about writing to me. Or even about coming back here."

Mrs Kershaw put her arms around Linda and embraced her.

Putting her head on her mother's shoulder, Linda sighed. "I love him so much. Only I haven't told him so."

Her mother held her away, looking into her face. "Does he love you? Has he told you?"

As Linda nodded, she said briskly, "Well then, if you can tell me, you can tell him — surely?"

Then she moved away swiftly. "I suppose I'll have to help you with these sandwiches or I'll never get my kitchen to myself. Then your father will be coming home and wondering why his dinner isn't ready!"

Linda had to smile.

The smile was still curving her lips as she went out a little while later with her anorak on and the hood up and her haversack slung over her shoulder.

Euan was waiting for her at the corner. His face lit up into a smile when he saw her.

As he hurried to meet her, Linda's heart was radiant. The rain did not matter to either of them.

She still did not know what the future would hold for them but as their smiles mingled and their eyes beamed out dazzling signals of love, they were securely wrapped in a wonderland of enchantment. □

THE MAGIC OF THE YEARS

by PHYLLIS HEATH

ANNE MAYBURY lifted the lid of the old trunk and sat back on her heels as the musty smell of its contents reached her nostrils.

It must have been five or six years since she'd last looked inside it, and much, much longer since it had been used for its original purpose. When Carol, her eldest daughter, had gone to college she had looked in horror at the ancient trunk, preferring to use a large suitcase and a lot of cardboard boxes to transport her possessions.

A fan, its bright colours dimmed, caught her eye and she lifted it tenderly. She'd brought it back from that first holiday in Spain with Bob. That had been before the children began to come along — Carol, Tony and young Kate.

Kate!

Anne dropped the fan hurriedly. Her 17-year-old daughter would soon be home! And she'd be expecting to see what her mother had found in the way of an outfit for the college dance.

"We're all dressing up in old clothes. No, not old, *old.*" The girl had laughed, seeing her expression. "We had a Tramps' Ball last year. This time we've settled for 'Days Gone By,' " she said, putting the words in inverted commas. "You must have lots of things I could alter to fit me, Mother," she had told Anne candidly.

Kate was slim as a willow and Anne took the remark resignedly.

I'm plump. I've always been plump . . . pleasingly plump. She chuckled, remembering the way her husband, Bob, used the description advancing threateningly towards her, his eyes gleaming wickedly. "Very, very pleasing," he would whisper as he hugged her close.

Still smiling, Anne began to lift out the contents of the trunk, determined to keep her mind on the task and not go wandering down memory lane.

A pale blue, flimsy evening dress came first. She'd fondly imagined it made her look like one of the lovely young women who paraded down sweeping staircases in musicals.

Next, a white summery dress with a huge collar and cabbage roses. Right up to date in the Fifties, Anne recalled.

She laid this aside gently. It was the dress she'd been wearing when

The Magic Of The Years

Bob proposed and it conjured up all the sweet agonies of falling in love.

Perhaps she could use it. Perhaps the magic would work for Kate, too.

Kate was in love. And she was just the age Anne had been.

She could recognise all the signs. The long silences, the babble of words after, punctuated by Malcolm. The dashes to answer the telephone, and the breathless sighs . . .

There had been boys before but, clearly, this one mattered and the coming dance was the event Kate was counting on to bring things to a head.

Quickly she pushed the rest of the things into a waste sack, eager to put them out of sight before she relented. Then her fingers felt the softness of velvet and she didn't need to examine her find to know what it was.

"Mrs Tilsley's jacket," she breathed, shaking out its folds.

Its once white lining was yellowed with age, and perhaps because it had lain nearly 30 years in the trunk. The cord, twisting down the front, needed a stitch or two and the high collar was greasy and smudged. Probably with make-up, Anne thought, remembering when last it had been worn.

The frog fastening was firmly anchored where Mrs Tilsley had sewn it. Yes, she'd been plump at 16, even more so than now — which was why Mrs Tilsley had had to add the fastener when the row of neat black buttons wouldn't reach.

Anne's expression softened as she thought of the elderly woman who had taught the fifth form the rudiments of sewing. Brought back to teaching during the shortage which followed the war, she was unfitted to control this new generation. The girls had treated her with the sort of affection one bestows upon a puppy.

She was a good teacher, though, Anne thought. And she knew her job.

It was this which had brought the jacket to the notice of the fifth form. Mrs Tilsley couldn't forget the war years, with their policy of make-do and mend, and many a parent blessed her when her pupils raided their wardrobes for old garments.

"Things go in circles, my dears," the elderly woman told them. "Everything comes round again, like the sun. What's the latest fashion in sleeves?"

They had tried to sketch with their hands and she'd cried triumphantly: "Leg o' mutton! That's what they were called when I was a girl. Narrow at the wrist, full at the top. I'll bring the jacket I have, with sleeves like that."

IT had been the black velvet jacket Anne was holding and she recalled the tender way the teacher had spread it for their inspection. With a flash of insight she had seen that this garment meant a lot to Mrs Tilsley.

She lingered when most of the others had left the classroom. "It's beautiful, Mrs Tilsley."

"Yes, my dear. More than that."

Anne nodded, not needing the soft words to be explained.

A voice spoke behind her: "Would you lend us the jacket? For the play. It's just the thing for Anne's part."

The teacher's eyes flicked to Anne. "Would you like it? Is it suitable?"

Before Anne could speak, Anthea answered. "Oh, yes, Mrs Tilsley. It'd be just right. And the play is for charity, for disabled soldiers, you know."

"I'd forgotten that." Mrs Tilsley smiled. "In that case . . . come to the staff-room later, Anne, and we'll see what can be done to help."

From being somewhat reluctant, the teacher had become quite enthusiastic. She greeted Anne warmly.

"I've been reading the play, my dear, and Anthea's correct, it is the right period. You'll look quite handsome in it."

She pulled ineffectually at the front edges.

"I'm afraid we were all rather skinny when I was a girl. But we'll make it right."

She patted the part of Anne which shouldn't have shown between the edges of the jacket. "A crocheted cord, I think, and two buttons. Jet ones would be fine. Leave it to me, dear."

There was no mirror but Anne could guess how she looked. She cringed at the thought of appearing on stage like that, before the whole school and all the parents.

"But it means a lot to you. I'd be scared of spoiling it."

"Yes, but memories aren't everything. In a way it's fitting that it should help you make a success of the play.

"You see," Mrs Tilsley hesitated, "I wore that jacket when I watched John, my husband, go off on the embarkation train. He never came back, my dear."

Anne swallowed. What Mrs Tilsley had told her only made things worse.

"It's too precious," she began, but the teacher wouldn't listen.

"It's what you need and I'll be proud for you to wear it," she told Anne.

Two tears trickled down Anne's face now as she recalled the anguish that jacket had caused her.

When the fastening was sewn in place and she tried it on, she stared at herself, horrified. It looked worse than she'd imagined. Even with the rest of her costume there was no disguising that it was too tight and she was too fat for it. In fact, the puffed sleeves made her look even wider than ever.

After the dress rehearsal, when everyone told her how right the jacket had been, she knew she couldn't tell them how she felt.

I'll be sick, she decided. I won't be in the stupid play. I won't be laughed at.

When everyone had had their say, Anthea eyed Anne maliciously.

"Sooner you than me." She laughed. "You look like a great black sausage that's bursting out of its skin."

Anne gritted her teeth. "You couldn't wear it, because you can't act, Anthea Crawley. It isn't me that's wearing the jacket, it's the character I'm playing."

ONCE again Anne brushed the tears from her eyes. Sounds downstairs told her Bob had come home.

Stupid, middle-aged fool, she chided herself. Fancy sitting here crying over some childish humiliation!

Crushing the velvet between her hands, she reached for the waste sack as Bob stepped into the room.

"Hello! What are you doing sitting alone in the dark?" he said.

"I didn't realise it had got so dark," Anne said, glad for a moment to cover her confusion.

Bob switched on the light and came towards her. "What have you got there? Don't I remember this?"

He took the jacket from her, holding it up and looking at it.

A reminiscent smile came to his lips. "Yes, I do know it. You wore it in that play. I don't think it would fit you now," he teased.

"Not that it exactly fitted you then." He smiled, showing he hadn't forgotten. "It belonged to that little woman who took us boys for scripture and you girls for sewing, didn't it?

"Did you know that she sat through that play with the tears running down her face? Not crying, really, my mother told me, but she made no attempt to wipe them away. We weren't that bad, were we?"

Anne shook her head. "It wasn't us. It was the way she felt, her memories."

"I guessed it was something like that, especially with the coat being so old. But it put me off a bit, when I first came on stage and saw her on the front row crying. After a bit I forgot all about her. Do you remember how I forgot my lines and you kissed me so you could whisper in my ear?

"You were an old softy even then," he said, pulling her to her feet and into his arms.

"You only wore that preposterous jacket because that old dear wanted you to. I heard them teasing you at rehearsal, but you stuck out and said you'd wear it for her sake. I think that was when I first fell in love with you."

ROBERT!" Surprise made Anne use his full name. "I'd loved you for ages!

"Well, ever since the beginning of that term. That was what made it all so awful. I knew I would look a frump, a fat frump, just when I wanted to make an impression. I'd dreamed of playing opposite you, imagining you telling me how wonderful I'd been. You didn't say a word," she added reproachfully. "I don't think you noticed I was around."

"I could hardly help but notice you in that get-up." Bob laughed, but he kissed her. First on her lips and then where the tears had smeared the dust on her cheeks. Anne realised he'd known all along how she'd been feeling.

Bob touched her stained cheeks gently. "I couldn't have been so happy with anyone but you, Anne. You do know that, don't you?"

He rocked her gently in his arms and she buried her face in the familiar scent of his jacket.

I'll make something for Kate from that blue dress, she decided. And clean up the jacket. It will fit her, without the frog fastening, and it will look lovely over the dress when she's walking home with Malcolm.

Perhaps Mrs Tilsley was right. Perhaps everything just goes on going round and round, even love. That jacket brought Bob and me all this happiness; perhaps it will give Kate a helping hand, too. □

A S Don walked out of the little local airport he drew a deep breath. The air was just as he had know it would be — crisp and cool, with just a suggestion of sea-salt in it. The freshness of the air in his homeland was one of the things he had missed most during his tour of duty overseas.

Other unpleasantries like temperatures in the hundreds, poverty and perpetual frustration hadn't affected him nearly so deeply as the lack of freshness in the air.

Even the company cars had been air-conditioned, and he remembered the shock received on winding down a window on a particularly fetid day — a hot blast of air had almost singed his face.

"The Lu wind," his driver had explained with a deprecating grin.

He had been tempted to return home during his mid-term leave but he had resisted temptation and had gone to Agra to see the Taj Mahal.

It was magnificent, of course, as was the rose-pink city of Jaipur and the lakes of Kashmir, but none of them had brought him the peace of mind

So Dear The Memory

by Gay Wilson

which he sought, and his restlessness increased with the passing months.

If only Valerie had been by his side! Then the whole tour would have been an exciting adventure. Valerie with her bright, observant eyes, her eager, enquiring mind and her bubbling high spirits. But Valerie had opted for duty instead of love, and his heart had been filled with bitterness.

He remembered how he'd pleaded with her.

"Surely you could find *someone* to look after your mother. You can't let me go out to India alone?"

"Who, for instance?" she'd retorted.

"Well . . . a nursing home . . . or something. She'd be well looked after in a nursing home."

But Valerie had shaken her dark head so vigorously the hair had danced like silken tassels.

"She'd hate it!" she cried. "It would kill her. How can you suggest such a thing?" And she'd burst into stormy tears.

He'd apologised abjectly, but later he'd tried again. He couldn't bear the thought of losing her and there didn't seem to be any other way out.

"What about us?" he urged. "What about your promise to me? Why should you sacrifice your life to your mother?"

"It may not be for long," she'd pleaded. "The doctors say not . . ."

"But she's had her happiness. It isn't fair."

"Life isn't fair," Valerie said bleakly. "Whoever said it was?" She gave a deep sigh and her eyes went dark with emotion.

"Please try to understand, Don. It's not that I don't want to come to India with you as we planned, it's because I can't.

"I couldn't live with myself knowing I'd abandoned Mother in some home for the elderly. She'd feel forsaken, and I think she'd die. It would spoil my life; it would spoil both our lives. I'd keep thinking about her and worrying. You see, she's a loner, she would never settle."

"Then I won't go," he'd stated flatly. "It's not worth all the hassle. I'll turn down the assignment." He pulled her into his arms and tried to kiss away their joint unhappiness, but she pulled away fiercely.

"I won't let you!" she cried. "How d'you think I'd feel perhaps years later, knowing I'd spoiled your career? This is your big chance, Don; you've told me so yourself. You have to take it."

SOMBRELY Valerie took the sapphire ring from her finger and pressed it into his reluctant hand.

"You will meet someone else." Her voice was quiet but determined and a terrible desolation filled his heart for he realised he could not move her. Many times in the past he'd admired her strength of character, her definition of right and wrong, and in this — her testing time — he knew she would not falter.

"Keep the ring," he begged miserably, almost in tears himself. "Keep it for friendship's sake."

There was a sad little twist to her mouth as she shook her head.

"I feel more than friendship for you, Don. I always have." Her stubborn, no-nonsense little chin jutted out as she spoke, and he felt he had never loved nor needed her so much as at that painful moment.

"We'll keep in touch, though, won't we?" he pleaded.

"Of course," she said gently, as if addressing a frightened child.

For a year or two letters had passed between them. Bright, chatty, unsatisfying letters, where hope rose and was crushed. And then gradually they ceased as Mrs Duncan sickened and rallied and lingered on.

Gradually their correspondence petered out, and the only news he heard was through his own mother.

"Mrs Duncan is frail but very cheerful. Valerie is an angel and a slave. I hope you are meeting some nice young girls in Chasnallah."

But there weren't any nice young girls in Chasnallah. It was a mining area of great poverty where he was working on the modernisation of a coal mine. Any nice young girls there may have been were in the cities or up in the hills.

Even there the girls were few and far between, and the rather withdrawn, sombre-faced young engineer didn't appeal to them any more than they appealed to him.

A ND then when the strain was beginning to tell, came news of his parents' impending Ruby Wedding.

"Your mother refuses to have a celebration party unless you can come home for it," wrote his father. It was the opportunity he had subconsciously been waiting for. The face saving opportunity to go home.

He wrote to them promising to arrange his next leave to suit, and then went off to Calcutta for a few days to do some shopping. He knew exactly what he wanted for an anniversary present, and he was almost certain it could be obtained in the famous New Market there.

He found it the second day! A glowing Kashmiri hearthrug in ruby, pink and cream which he could visualise in front of the old stone fireplace at his home, and he knew his mother, at least, would treasure it.

After arranging for the despatch of the rug, he made arrangements for his homeward flight, and his heart beat high with uncrushable hope that fate might after all be kind to him.

They were all at the little airport to meet him. He had crossed Heathrow alone and it had been bleak, but here were his parents, Jenny, his sister and wee Neil, who had been in a pram when he left.

"Kevin is waiting in the car," Jenny said when the hugs and kisses were over, and his mother and father stood smiling and half-crying at the same time.

After the first exuberance of the family re-union was over, he drew his mother aside and enquired about Valerie.

"She's still as tied as ever," she told him sadly. "Her mother is a complete invalid now, and doesn't get out of her bed. We don't see anything of them.

"Valerie did send an embroidered picture for the wedding, but I doubt if she'll come to the party."

The Ruby Wedding Celebration was a huge success. Friends and relatives poured in bearing gifts and good wishes. There was scarcely room for the couple! Jenny had made a cake with ruby red hearts on it, and there were dark red roses in profusion all over the house. The Kashmiri rug arrived on time and was the object of much comment and admiration.

Photographs were taken, champagne drunk, and reminiscences were the order of the day. Don set himself out to be charming and helpful, and few noticed the sad expression in his eyes.

Valerie didn't come to the party. He hadn't really expected her. He was afraid she might be different from the picture he carried in his heart; and even more afraid she might be the same.

It was over five years now since they had parted, and it was inevitable that they had both changed.

He felt he was hanging on to a pipe dream, but he couldn't dispel it. He longed to take the short drive over to her house, but he couldn't bring himself to do it.

If she'd wanted to see him, surely she could have come to the party if only for an hour. What was there to discuss?

And yet his heart refused to give up hope. Something might turn up, he told himself, and he had two more weeks of leave yet.

Something did turn up! It was an announcement in the deaths column of the local paper.

"Mrs Duncan's died!" his mother exclaimed, peering more closely to ensure that she hadn't made a mistake. "That poor girl. I wonder if she was all on her own?"

He snatched the paper and read the announcement for himself.

"It was last week!" he cried. "The funeral was yesterday." His eyes blazed in his white face. "I must go to her at once . . ."

"Do you think you should?" his mother cautioned. "Why not ring first? She could have let us know, but she didn't."

He stared at her impatiently.

"She'd be too upset to do that," he said. "May I borrow your car, Mum?"

"Yes, dear, of course," she said, but she still looked worried. "Do be careful of intruding. It's years since you and Valerie were sweethearts, and she's very proud. Don't be . . . precipitate . . ."

But he'd gone; flinging on his jacket as he went.

DON remembered it all so well. The winding lane which led to Valerie's house. The little school where she'd started her first teaching job. The church beside the burn, the dilapidated riding school, and finally, the ivy-covered house where the Duncans had lived for more than a generation.

The garden was as neat as he remembered it. Geraniums and blue ageratum in the tubs on the porch. Delphiniums, phlox and lupins in the beds, and the small lawn he had re-shaped for them so long ago.

The windows of the house were wide open, and he thanked God it appeared she was at home.

Valerie answered the door herself, and they stood looking at each other in silence for a couple of seconds. Then she seemed to crumple, and would have fallen if he had not moved to catch her in his arms. "I only heard this morning," he said, cradling her head into his shoulder. "Oh, Val! Oh, darling, what can I do to help you?"

"Just . . . hold me . . ." She sobbed.

AFTERWARDS, Don made tea and brought it to her, supporting her as she sipped the hot liquid. Her tears were easier now, but he could feel her shivering.

He looked around for something to cover her with, and seeing nothing, peeled off his sweater, draping it across her shoulders and tying the sleeves beneath her chin.

"It's . . . it's the one I knitted for you," She smiled through her tears. "I thought it would be worn out long ago."

"Sweaters last a long time in my part of India," he said. "I didn't wear it at first — I couldn't . . ."

"I didn't mean to make you unhappy, Don." Her tears flowed afresh. He stroked her hair.

"I was selfish," he said. "I should have been more understanding. I was only thinking of myself." He lifted her chin and bending his head kissed her lips with gentle penitence. "Can you forgive me?"

Her arms crept round his neck then, and words were unnecessary between them. The silence lasted for several minutes, and although there were things he desperately needed to ask her, he forced himself to hold his peace.

Suddenly the doorbell rang. Valerie sat up slowly, pushed the hair away from her forehead, and blew her nose.

"It'll be Mrs Anderson," she said. "She's been so good to me while Mother was ill."

He tried to remember Mrs Anderson from the old days, but failed. She turned out to be plump, elderly and a trifle bossy.

"She should be resting," she told Don severely. "She's worn out."

The implication was so obvious he had no recourse but to take his departure.

"I'll be back," he whispered as Valerie let him out of the front door. "I'll ring you first thing in the morning."

He kissed her with a new gentleness, and then he was striding down the garden path, his mind in a state of chaos. What was he going to do? He had to be back on the job in less than two weeks, yet how could he leave this darling, grief-stricken girl at a time like this?

He wondered if it would be possible for him to extend his leave, but knew it was very doubtful. The work overseas was now in full swing, and he had heavy responsibilities.

He would have dearly loved to have thrown up the whole job which had caused so much suffering, but he knew how high unemployment was at home and there could be no certainty of him getting a job.

A husband on the dole would be no use to Val, no matter how much he loved her.

He put his mother's car into gear and drove off jerkily. So deeply engrossed was he in his troubled thoughts he completely failed to see the van emerge from behind a parked lorry, and the next thing was a sickening crunch. The car seemed to fold like a concertina and he felt an agonising pain in his left leg, and then blackness.

THE sun was shining in through an open window when Don woke up. There was a bowl of ruby red roses on a small table beside his bed, their perfume almost obscuring the smell of antiseptic in the room. He tried to move, but pain shot through him, and he saw that his left leg was suspended in a pulley arrangement above his bed. He dimly remembered being involved in the accident.

The door opened and a pleasant-faced nurse wearing a blue and white uniform came into the room.

"That's better," she remarked cheerfully. "You're really awake this time. I'll fetch your wife. She's still in the waiting-room and must be exhausted, poor little thing."

"I don't have a wife." He tried to say the words, but no sound escaped and the nurse went on chatting.

"You've broken your leg in two places, and had severe concussion. But you'll be OK in a week or so. You're a very lucky young man. Your car was a write-off."

She plumped his pillows and straightened his sheets, checked that there was water in the jug on the bedside table.

"I'm sorry I can't make you any more comfortable at the moment," she apologised, "but I'll send your wife in."

And then Valerie was standing beside him, looking small and frightened and desperately weary. He tried to be nonchalant.

"They tell me you're my wife!" he murmured.

"I . . . I told a white lie," she stammered. "They mightn't have let me see you otherwise." She dabbed her eyes and blew her nose. "I thought I'd lost you too, Don."

He was still terribly hazy, but he was determined to keep her talking somehow. She might disappear if he didn't. He forced his eyes to open . . .

"I'm fine . . ." he lied.

Later his parents came, but when they saw Valerie, they refused to stay more than a few minutes.

"How did you find out I was in hospital?" he asked her when they were alone once more.

"Your folk phoned me when you didn't arrive home. It was dreadful — we couldn't find out how badly you were injured. But you're going to be fine . . ."

He was well on the road to recovery when they finally talked about themselves.

"I'd give anything not to have to go away again," he told her miserably.

"But you're not fit!"

"Indian hospitals are pretty efficient nowadays. They'll be able to cope with a leg in plaster, and I can still sit at a desk. I shall be able to get around the site, too, in a week or so. I have to get back as soon as the doc. allows it."

He stroked her hand as it lay on the sheet. Such a small capable hand, completely free of jewellery.

"May I give you back your ring?"

His eyes were gravely appealing and had a gentle expression she had never seen before. Her face flamed and then paled.

"You still have it?"

"Of course. Get my jacket, love; it's in the cupboard." She obeyed him, returning with the jacket, and laid it across the bed. He fumbled with a small inside pocket, his eyes never leaving her face as he withdrew a jeweller's box.

"It's too big now," she said, as he slipped it on her finger. "I must have shrunk." Tears filled her eyes.

"I'll get it fixed," he said. "The first thing I'll do when I get out of here is to have it fixed. We'll go back to Simpsons together."

She twisted the ring round and round her finger. It was very slack.

"Don," she whispered, "promise not to be angry, but I can't face getting married just yet. There's so much to do. Please understand." Her voice was gently adamant.

"I do understand, my darling. For you I'm prepared to wait for ever. Before I go back I'll help you all I can with paperwork and whatever." He put his hand over hers.

When he spoke again his voice was vibrant with tenderness.

"Could you face a Christmas wedding, Val? Here in the church down the road?"

For a moment the lost brightness illuminated her sad face.

"How could that be, Don?"

"I shall apply for special leave," he said eagerly. "Compassionate leave. I think I'll be lucky, especially as I'm returning covered in plaster this time. My boss is very fair." He drew her into his arms and held her close. "We could honeymoon in Kashmir. I know exactly the right place to stay."

Suddenly he felt her relax. She gave a little sigh of contentment, and it seemed that a current of sympathy and complete understanding flowed between them at last, which made words unnecessary. □

SHONA awoke in the pale light of a Hebridean dawn, with her grandfather's words still ringing in her sleep-dulled mind.

"I'll not go to the mainland, Shona. I know your father brought you here to persuade me, but I'll not go."

Shona had listened and said nothing. She had been too tired after the long journey from Aberdeen to argue with the old man. Anyway, she had seen little point — she knew too well that stubborn set of jaw and the hard glitter in his eyes.

Shona sighed, threw back the covers and climbed out of bed. She crossed to the window, her bare feet cold on the polished floor. Pulling back the curtains and bending to look through the low window at mist shrouded hills, she forgot for a moment the purpose of her visit, forgot everything but the beauty of a Skye morning, the first she had spent on the island in two years.

It had been dark when the Land-Rover had bounced across the final few miles to the outlying croft the previous night, and now Shona drank in the glory of the landscape that had been so much a part of her childhood.

The day was growing brighter, and the dark shapes of the Cuillins

by
Donna
Grice

towered arrogantly above the glen, dwarfing the crofts and houses. Spring growth had softened the foot hills with new green, but the barren mountains remained black and forbidding. It might have been spring on the low ground, but winter lingered as a shining crown of snow marking the summits of the higher peaks.

No-one else was up yet, and with only the distant sound of a cuckoo's morning song to keep her company, she dressed and quietly left the house.

Away from the tiny rooms of her grandfather's house, in the freedom of the fresh morning, her spirits lifted slightly. Taking the path round the back of the house, she turned her steps up the hill towards the sea cliffs. The sheep-cropped turf felt soft and springy beneath her feet after the unyielding pavements of Aberdeen. The higher she climbed the more at ease she felt. A fresh breeze sprang up, coming off the sea at the turning of the tide, blowing away the last vagrant remnants of mist from the hollows of the land.

She reached the top of the hill, breathless from the climb, legs aching with the unfamiliar exercise. With the sun warm on her back she sat on an outcrop of rock, looking out over the cliff where wild Atlantic water broke its journey.

The Heart Needs No Reason

As a child, this was the place she had come to when something troubled her, and in the free wild air she had found clarity and reason. Her mind drifted back over the years to the holidays spent roaming the hills with her grandfather and his dog. To the evenings by the fire, sitting on his knee, snuggled into the protective curve of his arm.

He had always seemed old to Shona. Old and yet ageless, unchanging. His face was brown and wrinkled like leather, with blue eyes that sparkled when he smiled at her. He loved the land with a fierce pride, and he had tried to teach Shona to love it.

THE sound of a gull calling overhead brought Shona back to the present. The smile faded from her lips as childhood memories receded, and she thought about the argument that had set father against son.

Living with her parents in Aberdeen, she knew how much her father worried about old Alasdair. And yet, since Shona's grandmother had died, five years previously, he had managed very well on his own.

But he was 72 now, and his son, Alec, had an eye to the future.

Time and again he had asked old Alasdair to move to the mainland to be closer to his family, each time becoming more insistent. And each time old Alasdair had refused, quietly but firmly. This time Alec had brought Shona to try to persuade her grandfather to move — Shona, Alasdair's only grandchild, his joy.

There seemed to be no way out. Both her father and grandfather were stubborn and refused to give an inch, and Shona was stuck in the middle, not knowing what to do.

She turned her head to the sound of a dog barking along the cliff top.

Its master came into view, and even from a distance, Shona recognised his big frame and easy walk. The man and the dog drew level with her and stopped, the dog nuzzling her hand affectionately.

"How are you, Hugh?" Shona smiled up at the shepherd.

"Oh, I'm the same as ever. Bess and I don't change, do we, girl?" He stooped to scratch the dog's ear gently with his rough hand. "It's good to see you again. You're up on the hill early, though."

"It's such a lovely morning, too nice to miss." Shona looked out across the sea. "I haven't seen any eagles yet, Hugh. Have they gone?"

"No, there's a few from time to time. They're no bother to the sheep, though, just take a weakling lamb now and then that would be dying anyway. It's the hoodies and the black-backs I've no time for. Evil birds they are, cruel for the sake of it. They'll have the eyes from a new-born lamb just for the sport."

Hugh was well launched into his favourite subject, the land, and the sheep in his care that roamed across it. For nearly half a century he had walked the hills with his dogs, minding his animals. Shona sat back and listened, enthralled by his knowledge of all the island's creatures, letting the Gaelic lilt of his voice wash over her.

A FTER a time, Hugh stopped talking and Shona looked up to find his shrewd eyes watching her.

"Is there trouble between them?" He nodded towards the house down in the glen.

"Yes, Hugh, I'm afraid there is, and I don't know what to do about it, what I can say to help. I'm right in the middle."

"Old Alasdair taught me all I know about sheep." Hugh sighed. "He's as much a part of the land as they are. He belongs here, he won't leave."

"I know that, but my father won't see it. Besides, I really don't know who's right. Dad has a point, you know."

"That's as may be, but he'll never move old Alasdair from the island, you'll see." Hugh laughed. "Besides, he's not so much on his own as your father seems to think. He has friends if he needs them.

"Go down to the house now . . . doubtless your father will be wondering where you are. I'm away up the hill to check the lambs." He looked up at the few stray clouds blowing in from the sea. "I don't like the feel of the weather this morning. It's not too late for snow yet."

He whistled to Bess and she was instantly on her feet by his side, and together they moved inland across the high moor.

Shona watched them until they were no more than spots of colour on the hillside. Then she turned towards home, walking slowly down the hill, leaving the clifftop to the screaming gulls.

Walking round the side of the house, the smell of frying bacon and the sound of raised voices spilled out of the open door to meet her. She took a deep breath and went inside, and the two men stopped arguing. An uneasy quiet settled on the kitchen as they all sat down to breakfast. Shona did her best to make conversation, but her words fell like stones into the silence.

"I saw Hugh up the hill," she said brightly. "He's just the same as I remember him."

"Oh." Old Alasdair grunted. Shona's father continued eating his breakfast with exaggerated concentration.

"He thinks the weather will turn soon," she continued.

At this, old Alasdair looked up with interest.

"Does he now?" He turned to look out of the window and frowned. "Well I dare say he knows what he's talking about."

HUGH was right. By midday the sky was a boiling mass of dark clouds and the wind had risen to a howl, shrieking under the roof and throwing squalls of rain against the window panes.

Old Alasdair began to pace the kitchen, stopping occasionally to look out of the window towards the high moor and shake his head. Blackie lay curled up on the rug by the fire, ever watchful of his master, his grey muzzle twitching as an outhouse door banged in the wind.

"I'm going to fix that door," Alec said impatiently. "I can't stand that banging all day long." Shona looked up from her book as he pulled his coat on and went out, slamming the door behind him.

"That son of mine always did have a temper," old Alasdair said.

"He worries about you a lot," Shona replied.

"Well, he's no need to. So don't you start on that tack again, Shona." She smiled at him.

But her smile faded as he took his coat from the hook behind the door and whistled softly to Blackie.

"Where are you going, Grandad?"

"Out on the hill. Where else?"

"In this weather! You'll catch your death of cold," she protested.

"Now don't take on so. I've been out in worse than this. Hugh will need some help with the lambs. There'll be snow before the day's out."

"Then let me come with you."

Old Alasdair paused with his hand on the latch and his expression softened.

"No, lass. You stay here and see that there's food for us when we get back. And don't let your father come after me. He doesn't know his way round these hills like I do."

With that he was gone, and Shona went to the window and watched as his figure was swallowed up by the murky afternoon. She thought she heard Blackie give one bark, but it could have been the wind, and she shivered as the first hard flakes of snow tapped at the window.

Her father was angrier than she had ever seen him when he came in from mending the door.

"Of all the stupid things to do," he ranted. "Doesn't he realise he's too old now to be tramping round the hills in a blizzard chasing sheep?"

Shona knew better than to answer him. She busied herself making a stew, and left her father to stare angrily into the fire.

He'll be all right, Shona kept telling herself as she listened to the storm raging outside. She had been repeating the words to herself all afternoon, and now it had been dark for an hour and the storm was at its height. Her ears ached with the noise of it, and even the snug little kitchen seemed cold and damp.

Alec looked at his watch every few minutes and had been to the door several times to look out. But beyond the small pool of light that the open door cast on the snow-covered ground all was a seething darkness. The storm was all-powerful.

Shona and he hardly spoke, they didn't need to voice the concern they felt.

The constant howling of the wind dulled Shona's senses, and eventually she dozed in the chair by the fire. The distant sound of a barking dog woke her, and instantly she was on her feet, following her father to the door. They stood together, looking out into the storm, and saw shapes emerge from the swirling snow. Two tall figures bent against the wind, with two smaller ones cowering at their feet.

And then the kitchen seemed to be full of noise and people. There were three lambs, two dogs and two men to be dried and fed, amid plenty of talking and laughing.

At last Hugh and old Alasdair were in dry clothes, with a dram of whisky inside them, sitting down to steaming dishes of Shona's stew.

Shona sat back, listening to the men talking, and watching her grandfather's face. He looked tired but happy, his eyes glowing with achievement. The age-old battle had been fought again, man against the elements, and Shona knew that old Alasdair was rightly savouring the taste of victory.

She glanced at her father. He was looking at old Alasdair, too, and all the anger had gone from his face. A smile hovered round his mouth as he listened to the two men talking of the day's work.

"It was wild up there today, Hugh. I thought we'd lost those ewes up on the bluff, and if it hadn't been for the dogs, well . . ." Old Alasdair shook his head.

"Blackie's still a good dog for the sheep, Alasdair, old as he is."

Alasdair reached down and fondled Blackie's waiting muzzle.

"It has kept him going, doing the job he was born to. He's not a dog to be sitting out his last years by a fire." As he said this he didn't look at Hugh, but at his son, and Shona saw the look that passed between them and the slight nod of Alec's head.

Father and son smiled at each other before Alasdair turned back to his well-earned meal and Shona felt her heart lift. It's going to be all right, she thought. Dad understands now. There'll be no more talk about moving Grandad to the mainland.

Hugh's voice broke into her thoughts.

"There'll be some eagles about when the storm's over, Shona. You'll doubtless see them before you go home," he said, and winked at her across the table.

Shona smiled at him and sat back, warm in the contentment that now filled the tiny room. □

Printed and Published in Great Britain by D. C. Thomson & Co., Ltd., Dundee, Glasgow, London and Manchester. © D. C. Thomson & Co., Ltd., 1986.

ISBN 0-85116-342-4